FROM HERE

From Here
Lessons in Love & Loss from 9/11

by

Felice Zaslow

Brooklyn Soul Press

NEW YORK

Cover photo by Felice Zaslow.
Author photo by Ellen Wolff (www.ellenwolffphotography.com).

Cover and interior design by Schultz Yakovetz Judaica (www.schultzyakovetz.com).

Printed in the United States of America.

ISBN 979-8-9850271-1-2

CONTENTS

BOOK TWO: ... TO HEALING

To my parents, Lillian and Alfred, of blessed memory;
my sons, Bryan and Adam;
my grandchildren, Ithan, Dylan and Leor;
and Ira, the young man on the beach

P.S. 273　　　Felice Shea
Class 6-1　　June 6, 1961

What America Means To Me

This is not an easy question to answer but I can feel the answer in my heart as I walk along the street and see the little children playing.

There are people who are laughing and talking in small groups, cars are whizzing past me and I can hear the newsboy trying to sell his papers.

America means not only a place where I spend my time, but also a place where I live, where my father works in order to make a living, where I receive a careful and guided education, where I am growing up.

To my mind a good American is a person who stands up for his rights and a person who is willing to devote himself and his abilities to his country. As President Kennedy said at his Inaugural Address, "Think not of what your country can do for you, but of what you can do for your country."

Sixth grade essay from P.S. 273 (June 1961).

Preface

In the course of writing this book, I came across an essay I wrote in the sixth grade at P.S. 273 in Brooklyn, New York. Along with students across the nation, I was awarded a medal for Americanism and Patriotism from President John F. Kennedy.

"What America Means to Me"
This is not an easy question to answer, but I can feel the answer in my heart as I walk along the street and see the little children playing.

There are people who are laughing and talking in small groups, cars are whizzing past me and I can hear the newsboy trying to sell his papers.

America means not only a place where I spend my time, but also a place where I live, where my father works in order to make a living, where I receive a careful and guided education, where I am growing up.

To my mind a good American is a person who stands up for his rights, and a person who is willing to devote himself and his abilities to his country. As President Kennedy said at his Inaugural Address, "Think not of what your country can do for you, but of what you can do for your country."

That young girl in 1961 saw something she could believe in: a safe world, a reliable world and a promising future.

Prologue

What the world needs now is love, sweet love...

Jackie DeShannon's voice plays a continual loop in my thoughts. The combination of her sweet voice and the innocence of the words work like a magic elixir to my soul. Were these words naive when we heard them playing on our transistor radios in 1965? Yes, of course, they were. They were naive, simplistic. Foolish even. But in their simplicity, they also speak great truth and wisdom.

The world is a complex place. A dangerous place. A frightening place. It is also a place of incredible beauty and delight. And it is suffering.

We are suffering.

I understand this suffering intimately. On September 11, 2001, all the hatred, uncertainty and horror of the world visited me in a very personal way. My husband, Ira, worked in the World Trade Center. When he kissed me goodbye on that terrible morning, it was to be the last kiss I would ever feel from his lips.

The fog of that day, and the days that followed, is difficult to describe. The horror, so vividly shown on television, was echoed with deep dread and uncertainty in my soul. Hope did courageous battle against those devastating images. But the odds that Ira would be found alive and well were never good. Fortunately, during those first hours and days, I was operating on faith and not on the objective calculations of an actuarial. Still, the odds continued to shrink away as the days tumbled by, until there came a time when even I had to acknowledge that they had disappeared.

You cannot imagine how many times during those days that I clung to the fading sensory memory of his final kiss. My husband, the love of my life and the father of our two sons, was gone. Wiped out in an inexplicable expression of hatred, fear and murderous delight.

There have been volumes and volumes written about the experiences we all had that day. For so many, that day marked the end of their hopes, their innocence, the world as they understood it.

I believe with all my heart that there are no real endings. Transitions, yes. Changes, yes. But endings, no. There are moments that become the first of what is to come. But what is good and eternal can never be said to have a start and a finish. Losing Ira was the most painful experience of my life, but I know he would not want me or his sons to continue to suffer. He was too generous of spirit to want anything but our happiness. So, for his sake, and for ours, my family and I have had to go forward. We have had to find a way to heal.

In that regard, we are no different from any of the others who have suffered a terrible loss as the result of September 11th or, for that matter, anyone else who has had their life turned upside down by horrific tragedy and sadness.

"But how do you begin?" is a question that I am often asked by others when they confront a different future than the one they had imagined only hours, days and weeks before.

You begin with love.

You end with love.

We all need to heal. America cannot "undo" the horrors we experienced on September 11th. But we cannot allow ourselves to continue suffering.

I am not suggesting that those who still grieve should somehow hide or mask their hurt. Our grieving processes are very personal and follow different paths.

We need to find a way to go forward from hurt to healing. To go forward from here.

BOOK ONE

From Hurt...

CHAPTER ONE

Do You Believe in Magic?

It was June 1965. I had just turned sixteen. Do you remember what it was like to be sixteen in 1965? It was absolutely glorious! It's the time in a girl's life when the sun never again feels quite as warm and the secrets shared amongst girlfriends are never again so vital, when innocence seems as if it will last forever simply because she is completely unaware that she possesses it.

I had come down to Beach 23rd Street in Far Rockaway, New York, with a handful of friends, expecting nothing more than another perfect day on the beach, soaking up the sun, reading my book and talking with my friends.

These were the words I spoke at Ira's memorial service. Curious that I would begin with an innocent young girl, who was on the cusp of the next great phase of her life. At the time, of course, I had no way of anticipating what life held out for me next. All I was concerned about were the mundane needs of a life being lived for that brief moment in time.

My needs were simple. Friends. A book. Baby oil. A blanket. A transistor radio. The sand and sea…

"Who brought the blanket?" I asked.

"I've got it right here, as usual!" Ellen, one of my best friends, laughed.

We had a ritual that had come about quite naturally. On the first day of the summer, we had forgotten the blanket because everyone had thought that someone else would bring it. The next day, we *all* brought blankets. So, being the organized person I was, I assigned tasks. Ellen would bring the blanket. Dina would bring the radio. Janice brought some snacks. And I would bring the baby oil.

Every day after that when we arrived at the beach, I went through the checklist of things, and the answer was always the same—"I've got it right here, as usual!" It became something of a game.

We always sat on the same spot at Beach 23rd Street. Not too close but not too far from the ocean, well positioned to see our friends and spot cute boys. Of course, being sixteen, our thoughts were never far from spotting cute boys. Nothing was more exciting than when a boy we'd never seen before showed up on the beach. That could result in hours—or even days—of conversation.

Once we'd gotten to "our spot" on the beach, we would position ourselves on each side of the blanket so that we could lay it out nice and smooth on the sand. Then we laid our personal towels on the blanket. We smeared baby oil on our skin. Back then, we were only concerned with attracting the sun's rays and getting rich, dark tans. Like so many other dangers, concern about skin cancer or premature aging was beyond our youthful consideration. We wanted to fry in the summer sun!

While the others tended to get involved in conversation right away, I usually pulled a book out of my beach bag. I didn't go for typical beach "summer" reading. I would read books like *One Flew Over the Cuckoo's Nest, Catcher in the Rye* and collections by the Beat poets.

"Why do you always read those kinds of books?" Ellen asked me one day on the beach.

"I love these books," I said, holding up the copy of *Cuckoo's Nest* I was reading that day.

"I tried to get into that book one time, but it just depressed me," she admitted.

I shrugged. "I think it's wonderful. The writing is so powerful and the story is amazing."

"But it's about a bunch of patients in a mental hospital," she protested.

I shook my head. "It only seems to be about that. It's really about all of us and how we have to be brave and be willing to be a little different—to be ourselves—if we're ever going to be happy."

She shook her head. "You think too much, Felice. A pretty girl like you doesn't have to think so much."

I laughed. She was always saying things like that, mimicking the advice her mother was always giving her and us. She would say that we shouldn't worry too much about school. Just enough to stay interesting. Of course, that was advice that came right out of the 1950s. When we were seven and eight years old, still playing house, the advice seemed to make sense.

By the middle of the 1960s, that advice seemed almost quaint.

We never spoke about it, but we were all still stunned by the assassination of President Kennedy only two years earlier. That November day was as dark a day as any of us could remember in our young lives, and although we did not know it then, it portended a decade of turmoil.

Politics seemed faraway during the summer days on Rockaway Beach, but we were all aware of the changes happening in the world, in our world. Even in our innocence, we had already lived past the Cuban Missile Crisis and Kennedy's assassination. We were witness to the growing protests against the war in Vietnam. The college campuses across America seemed to be becoming hotbeds of protest. And the Civil Rights Movement affected each of us powerfully.

"Why don't you ever seem worried by all these things?" my mother asked me one time after the news had been on the radio.

I shrugged my shoulders. "Because I know that, no matter what, America will be all right."

I always knew that to be the case. I believed it with all my heart. During the darkest days of the war protests and the race riots that decade, I never had any doubt that we would find our way and do the right thing. I knew that no single politician's mistakes were great enough to veer America from her noble path.

Of course, these kinds of discussions only confirmed Ellen's concerns about my "thinking too much." No matter how hard I tried to convince her of the poetic vision of Kesey or the insight of Salinger, she preferred simple romances, romances that seemed to capture our mood on the beach so much better than the books I was reading.

On the particular day I remember now, we had settled in our spot at Beach 23rd Street and were just finishing up slathering the baby oil on our smooth skin when Ellen nudged me and pointed toward the breaking waves.

"Oh my God," she sighed.

"What?" I asked, squinting into the sunlight glimmering off the waves.

"Look at him," Janice said.

"Who?" I asked, shading my eyes with my hand and searching the shoreline.

"Him?" Dina asked, pointing in the same direction as Ellen.

"Don't point," Ellen said, "he'll see us."

"You were pointing," Dina said.

"That was before he was all the way out of the water."

"Who?" I demanded impatiently, dropping my book to my lap.

"Him," my three friends said in unison, looking toward the surf.

I turned to look in the direction they were facing and then I saw him too. There are moments that seem to jump out of the smooth motion of time and remain singular always. That moment was one. I remember it now as clearly as if it were still happening before my eyes.

"What the World Needs Now" had just begun to play on the transistor radio. Jackie DeShannon's breathy voice was dancing amongst the sounds of the beach, the pounding of the surf, the laughing and the talking of young people.

My friends and I had many conversations about the song. We all loved the song, but we were not in total agreement about what she was singing about. To my friends, Jackie was singing about romance—a thought never far from our minds. But I argued that she was singing about something larger, something to do with the troubles in the world. After all, we were beginning to confront such terrible issues in our world. From assassinations to war to college protesters to civil rights. It was beginning to seem that no one would ever get along. I believed that she was singing about the need for all people to simply get along with one another, to have relationships based on the most positive and most basic human emotion—love.

"Oh, you," Janice would tease me. "You're always thinking about important things like that."

But not on this day. On this day, with the song playing in the background, I was looking toward the surf with my friends as we all looked upon the beautiful young man emerging from the sea like some kind of mystical god.

"Oh my God, he's walking this way!" Ellen squealed in an excited whisper as she nudged me.

"I can *see* that," I whispered back, just as fiercely. "Do you think I'm blind or something?"

"Oh my God, oh my God," Janice and Dina said.

"Everyone just calm down," I said. I glanced at them to make it clear that I was serious. And then I raised my eyes back up. And there he was.

"Hi," he said.

"Hi," we all replied in unison, our voices no doubt giving away our enthusiasm at meeting him.

He smiled at us in that charming way teenage boys have of smiling at teenage girls, and we were all completely smitten. However, my feelings went deeper than simple infatuation. I *knew* the moment I saw him that he was the person I was meant to be with. Really.

I have always had a very deep sense of certainty when it came to such things. I believe that there is a deep order to the way we move through this world. My faith in this is complete. It is a faith I have carried from a very early age.

So it was no surprise to me that I was completely certain when I first met Ira that he and I would be together... even though I was not the first of my group of friends to date him. In fact, I didn't date him at all that summer. Janice and Ellen did.

I was matched that summer with Ira's cousin David. David, another charming, wonderful young man, had the simple misfortune

of following Ira out of the ocean that day and so being diminished by not being seen first.

"What's that?" David asked, looking down at the book in my hands.

"Felice is our resident intellect," Ellen said good-naturedly.

David leaned closer. "What are you reading?"

I held up the book, *Catcher in the Rye.*

"Is it any good?" David asked.

"It's great," Ira said, glancing over at his cousin.

"You've read it?" I asked him.

"Of course," he said. "Last year."

"I'm enjoying it," I told him.

And I was. Despite Holden's struggles, there was something about him and the book that enlivened me. There were times when I was reading it that I would sit on the beach and stare out at the ocean, allowing so many thoughts to go through my mind.

"What do you think of when you're staring like that?" Ellen asked me once.

I shrugged my shoulders. "I don't know. It's like I forget them as soon as I have them. It's like colors. It's just a nice sensation. Like something I can't quite remember but that I know is something wonderful."

Ellen shook her head. "I don't get you sometimes."

I smiled. "I don't get myself sometimes."

"But you're still wonderful," she added.

Summer! It was such a happy time.

The remainder of the summer I first met Ira consisted of meeting at the beach, going to parties, movies, diners and coffee shops. I discovered that I would likely never be a particularly good bowler, but I managed to have a good time lugging the heavy bowling ball to the top of the lane where I would send it on its way—inevitably to the gutter.

"Nice," Ira teased me gently after a particularly galling double gutter.

"Thanks," I smiled.

Not that any of my friends bowled any better! But it was fun and we got to enjoy the summer together. There were innocent make-out sessions and good-night kisses. We all felt so alive! Summer love! What could be more wonderful?

But, as other songs have warned, with the end of summer comes the end of summer loves. School began again and the dates ended. The leaves changed color and soon it was winter. The days grew shorter. There were tests to take and homework to finish. We still talked about boys, but we didn't have the free time to devote to our discussions.

I was a serious student, and I took my classes seriously. But even so, there were answers I just couldn't get at school—or anywhere else, as I came to learn. School is pretty good at answering the question, *How?* I was more interested in the question, *Why?* Even at my synagogue, I couldn't get quite the answer I was looking for. Too often, my questions were answered with "Because," or "That's the way it's always been" or something equally dissatisfying.

I knew there was a spiritual level of life that I couldn't quite tap into just yet, but I was certain that it was there. The 1960s were a great time for pseudo-spirituality, but that didn't attract me.

I think the increase in drug use had a lot to do with the search for spiritual understanding. Young people knew that there was something more to life than what they were experiencing, and they yearned to be a part of that. But they didn't know how to be a part of it, and the drugs made it seem easier.

Of course, they were wrong.

I was aware that The Beatles had gone to meditate with the Maharishi in India, but I wasn't interested in the media attention. I was interested in the truth itself. Meditation was a way to understanding. You didn't need television cameras or The Beatles to understand that.

During the next couple of years after that summer on the beach, I crossed paths with Ira a handful of times—most often when we were out on dates (with other people). We would see each other in line at a movie box office or skating at a skating rink. It was always nice to see him, even if we didn't speak much.

We didn't have to. I had the patience of someone who had been given knowledge. I knew Ira would be a good deal more in my life than a mere passing acquaintance. I don't think he had the same certainty at the time, but he sure recognized it in my face. More than once when we ran into each other, he would smile and ask me, "Why are you looking at me like that?"

"Like what?"

"I'm not sure, like you know something I don't."

I laughed. "I know lots of things you don't."

"Oh, really?" he would ask, rising to the friendly challenge. "Can you give me a for instance?"

But always, before I had a chance to give him an example, the push and pull of the evenings, our dates or something else interfered.

Until early spring 1969, that is.

CHAPTER TWO

The Birthday Present

Tempo dances at the Forest Hills Inn were almost *kibbutz* affairs—groups of friends meeting for fun. Romance was generally not a priority because we all knew each other so well for so long. However, before I turned twenty, in the days before spring, one particular dance turned out to be much different than any other.

The music was, by and large, fast and danceable. Sometimes, I danced with Ellen or Dina or Janice to The Isley Brothers' "It's Your Thing." Sometimes, we danced all four together to songs by Little Eva, The Temptations, and Sly and the Family Stone's "Hot Fun in the Summertime." Neil Diamond's "Sweet Caroline" always drew us onto the dance floor along with almost everyone else. However, about an hour into the dance, the band played an old song. It didn't have the same evocative power of the original singer's voice, but the words and the tune took me back to earlier summers and emotions.

"What the world needs now is love, sweet love…"

I couldn't help but smile to myself as the first notes of the song began to play. Suddenly, I became aware of someone behind me. I turned and I found myself face to face with a tall, dark-haired young man. I walked toward him, and before it registered who he was, I asked, "Do you have a cousin named David?" It was then that Ira realized who I was and broke out with one of his gorgeous, killer smiles.

"Care to dance?" he asked with a smile.

"When did you get here?"

He rolled his eyes, teasing me. "Do you always answer a question with a question?"

"Do you always sneak up on people?" I retorted with a smile.

"I guess I have my answer," he said as he extended his arms, inviting me to dance with him.

I accepted his "invitation" and moved closer to him. The combination of the song, his strong arms, the mood … everything … felt perfect. Although the song, like most songs then, was relatively short, while we were dancing it seemed to go on forever.

Of course, as soon as the song ended, it seemed to have ended much too soon.

"What have you been up to?" Ira asked me, as if we had broken off our most recent conversation only a day or two before rather than not having seen each other for a year or so.

"School." I looked around the room. "Dances."

He smiled.

"What have you been doing?"

"Out of school and working for Mobil Oil as a linear programmer."

I was still in college. Ira had finished graduate school and was employed in his first job. We talked about the war. About the draft. About what Ira would do if he was called up.

"It's not a moral war," he said.

"Is there such a thing?" I asked him.

He was thoughtful for a moment. "Of course, there is. There is never a *nice* war, but there are battles that must be fought. The Second World War is an example," he said. "Even Korea made sense. But Vietnam …" He made a face. "I don't think so."

I found his thoughtfulness powerful. Having "come of age" in the '60s, my almost reflexive reaction on the question of war and peace was always peace. However, Ira had introduced a difficult nuance that I could not ignore.

"The world is a very complex place. There aren't many simple answers to things."

"That's why I think that we must have a strong moral reason for moving forward," I argued.

"I agree. If it's only about power..."

We began a long conversation about "right and might" and the role of power in the world. Along the way, we touched on the importance of faith and spirit. Although I had not given it particular thought, the gorgeous young man who had come out of the ocean that summer's day four years earlier was a man of poetry and grace. I had not forgotten the feeling I had the first time I saw him, that he was the person I was meant to be with, but I hadn't had much time to dwell on it.

But somehow, on the dates I'd gone on and the boys I'd had crushes on, that was the measure they were weighed against—the unspoken bond that I had felt instantly when I saw Ira for the first time.

Only Ira managed to make the grade.

We must have been quite a sight that evening at the dance, standing in the middle of the dance floor not so much dancing as swaying together as we engaged in an intense conversation about the nature of war and peace, dignity and the morality of how people behaved toward one another.

Was communism always wrong? Was capitalism always right?

And what about America? Were *we* always right?

"For me, America is as much about ideas as about a real country," I told him. "The ideals of what we stand for..."

"I agree," he said. "I just think we sometimes slip between the ideal and the reality."

I smiled. "Don't we all?"

And then we were dancing again. I can no longer remember the songs we danced to, but I do remember that I didn't dance with anyone else that evening. When it was time to go home, Ira asked me for my phone number.

"You won't call," I teased him.

He looked at me seriously. "Haven't you been listening to me all evening?" he asked.

"What do you mean?"

"That's all I've been talking about, how I *would* call."

I was confused by his words but I knew perfectly what he meant. After all, we had talked about a great many things that evening, but the subtext was clear to both of us—we should be together.

True to his word, not long after I returned home from the dance, the phone rang.

"I've got it!" I called out as I darted toward the single phone in the apartment. Grabbing for the receiver, I lifted it anxiously to my ear. "Hello?"

"Hi."

It was him. "Hi."

"I had a great time at the dance."

"Me, too."

We then had the most inanely delightful conversation about nothing in particular, mostly about what we liked to do. I told Ira I liked to write, paint and travel, and he shared his love of skiing. The conversation ended with Ira asking me if I would like to go out with him. On a real date.

"Sure, that would be nice," I said, playing it cool.

"Sunday?"

"Sunday would be great."

I did not take note until later that Sunday would be the very first day of spring, the season of rebirth, of blossoming, of growth and joy. All I knew was that I felt like I was walking on air, waiting for Sunday to arrive.

Sunday was a perfect day. The air was warm. There was the scent of new flowers, early tulips and hyacinths starting to blossom in the air. As Ira walked up to the entrance of my building, the sun was still lighting the day.

He was unaware of being watched.

"Hmm, a sports jacket," my mother observed with an appreciative nod of her head. "Must be a nice boy."

My grandmother nudged my mother. "Lilly, this is it!" she said, her eyes never leaving Ira as he stepped up to the door and rang up to the apartment.

"Who is it?" my mother asked into the intercom.

I shot her a look. Who is it? She knew perfectly well who it was! She shrugged and smiled at me.

"It's Ira. I've come to pick up Felice."

"Oh, come right up."

As soon as she'd pushed the button to unlock the door, she turned to me and hurried me out of the room.

"What are you doing?" I wanted to know.

"Make it look like you're still getting ready," she said.

"But I am already ready," I protested.

She straightened up and looked me in the eye. "You like this boy?"

I nodded.

"Then go on into your room. I'll call for you when he comes in."

My sister, Michele, then sixteen, communicated her amusement at the interchange by opening her eyes wide and giving me "that look" that only siblings can share. It was just short of an eye roll. I grinned back in response, and we laughed.

"You be nice to him," I said over my shoulder as I headed for my room, although I knew already that my mother would be *very* nice to him.

I was listening from behind my door when the doorbell rang. I couldn't believe how fast my heart was beating as I listened to my mother and grandmother exchange pleasantries with Ira.

"Felice!" my mother called to me. "Ira is here."

Like I didn't know that? I drew in a deep breath and smoothed my dress. Then I opened the door. Ira looked up and smiled at me, and I felt the warmth of being smiled at by the man who would become the most important person in my life for the next thirty-two years. The intuitive "knowing" I had felt that summer of 1965 when Ira appeared on Rockaway Beach, I felt once again.

"Ready?" he asked.

I nodded as I smiled back at him.

"Nice meeting you," Ira said to my mother and grandmother.

I gave them both a kiss before leaving. As I bent to kiss my grandmother, she winked at me. "He's a nice boy."

From that first date, when we went to the movies and then dinner afterward, my mother and grandmother monitored every aspect of what they referred to as our "courtship."

"So? How are things going with Ira?" my mother would ask, her voice heavy with expectation.

"Fine," I'd answer honestly.

Actually, things were better than fine. The more time I spent with Ira, the more I knew we were made for one another. So much of the time, we seemed to know what the other was thinking. From our earliest dates, we could often complete the other's sentences, having similar thoughts about people, such as "I don't trust him," when I was thinking the same about a close friend's boyfriend.

"You and Ira seem to be getting very close," my mother might say in the evening, fishing for more information about our relationship.

"We're having a good time," I would answer.

I wasn't trying to be deceptive or hold my mother at bay. It was just that I was so much enjoying the balance I felt with Ira that I didn't want to do anything to upset it. I just wanted things to move along at their own pace.

We'd been going out steadily for nearly three months when my birthday came around in June. There was a great deal of talk in my apartment—none of it encouraged by me!—about what Ira might get me for my birthday.

"Maybe he won't get me anything," I said.

My mother made a face. "Of course he'll get you something. If he doesn't get you something, then it will be like saying that he doesn't really care for you. At least not in the way you care about him."

"He'll give her something," my grandmother intoned, her faith absolute on this particular point.

Ira took me out for a special dinner for my birthday, waiting until dessert to present me with my gift. I unwrapped the present carefully, and when I saw what it was, I couldn't have been happier.

After the date, I practically ran into the apartment, excited to show off my gift.

"A book?" my mother asked with mild disdain. "He got you a book? What? He couldn't have gotten you a nice bracelet?" She turned to my grandmother. "He got her a book. What does that mean, a book?"

My grandmother smiled and nodded. "A book. That's nice."

It was more than nice. As an English major, I valued books and literature far more than I did silly trinkets. Ira was deep and caring; he had poetry in his soul, and that poetry spoke to me. More than the choice of a book as a present was the particular book that he gave me—*The Prophet* by Kahlil Gibran.

Those pages spoke a wisdom and truth that seemed to echo the thoughts that had been taking form within me for years. I spent a great deal of time reading the pages of the book, and with each reading I marveled at the significance of this simple gift that Ira gave to me.

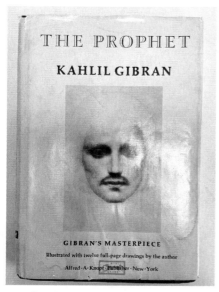
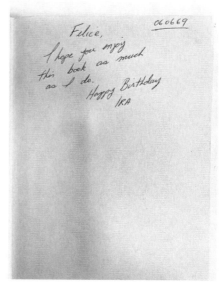

My first birthday present from Ira, June 1969

One passage in particular kept my attention, because it spoke to the future that I saw more clearly with each passing day:

Then Almitra spoke again and said, And what of Marriage, master? And he answered saying:
You were born together, and together you shall be forevermore.
You shall be together when the white wings of death scatter your days.
Ay, you shall be together even in the silent memory of God.
But let there be spaces in your togetherness,
And let the winds of the heavens dance between you.

Now, remembering the first time I read that passage, and the words that followed, I am startled by the power of the words. Of course, as a young woman in love, I thought I understood perfectly what Gibran had written. But now, as a woman who has experienced just such a marriage, I know too powerfully what it means when Gibran wrote, *"You shall be together when the white wings of death scatter your days. Ay, you shall be together even in the silent memory of God."*

CHAPTER THREE

The Twelfth of Never

There is another song from the 1960s, this one by The Rolling Stones, that begins with the words, *"Things are different today, I hear every mother say..."* That seems to me to be even more true now than it was then. Things are so different now. I have attended Bar and Bat Mitzvah celebrations that rival royal weddings. That wasn't the world that a girl from Brooklyn ever expected to encounter! For all its complexities, life was so much simpler then.

We were married on April 12, 1970. Two sets of parents with very little money could not stage the wedding of the century, but to us our wedding was the most magnificent ceremony ever, our *chuppah* (canopy) the most beautiful. We were married at the West Hempstead Jewish Center. I remember waiting in the bridal suite until it was time to walk down the aisle. The pre-wedding jitters I had experienced vanished the moment I proceeded down the aisle, both parents at my side. When I saw Ira waiting for me, ensconced in the light that streamed through the stained glass windows of the synagogue, I was at peace.

Our first dance was to the Johnny Mathis song "The Twelfth of Never."

When I close my eyes, I can still *feel* Ira's arms around me as we moved along the simple dance floor of the West Hempstead Jewish Center. Intellectually, I knew everyone was watching us, but in my heart and soul, it was as if we were alone. Just the two of us bound together in that eternal bond of love and life. The lines, "Melt my

On our wedding day, April 12, 1970

heart like April snow," and "Until the Twelfth of Never, I'll still be loving you," are forever etched in my memory.

Our early life together was a jumble of challenges and excitement. Every day was new, every achievement earth-shattering. We were building a life together, and every "brick" we placed formed part of the foundation of the life we shared. Movies we watched, books we read, friends we made and advancements we enjoyed professionally all added to the joy we shared together.

Not that every day was a honeymoon. We experienced the same ups and downs as every other couple. But each new challenge was met, and each met challenge made our relationship stronger.

As Ira often said, "We're in this together."

And we were. We made a good match. I liked to cook and he liked to eat. I was the one to seek out new adventures and he was happy to come along for the ride. We traveled to many places together or with friends, skiing at different mountains, exploring Europe, driving to Florida and around New York. He loved that I would talk and write about these excursions for days after. Sometimes he would tease me if he didn't play a big enough role in the retelling of the adventure, though.

"I *was* there too, wasn't I?"

"Of course!" I would agree. I would tell him he was like someone who only looked through photograph albums to find photographs he was in.

"There's something wrong with that?" he joked.

Ira was happy to do the things that I loved most. His own pleasures were simple and easy to accommodate. He liked his paddleball in the mornings. Regardless of my constant attention to the kinds of foods we ate, he always had to have his pizza break in the evening.

"A guy has to have pizza," he would claim. "After all, what is a day without a slice?" Pizza was either an appetizer or a snack for him. He would go on, pretending to be something of a statesman on the subject.

Of course, even with his daily pizza he managed to remain slim and enjoy the benefit of a naturally low cholesterol level. This made

The newlyweds in Flushing Meadows Park, Queens, New York

some of our friends envious, of course, especially as the years continued to roll by and more and more of us found ourselves sporting a little bit more on our thighs and stomachs than we would have liked.

But not Ira.

We were married five and a half years when our first son, Bryan Jonathan, was born. We were no longer just a married couple. And then, three years later, Adam Mathew was born. Now we were a family complete. And Ira was in his perfect element. He was a father to sons.

He was involved in every stage of their lives. From infants to toddlers to adolescents to young men, the relationship between them continued to mature. Ira reveled in their accomplishments.

How many summer evenings was he outside with them playing ball? How many conversations did they have about sports and the teams they loved? Their accomplishments were milestones in his life,

Family photo, from left: Adam, Ira, Bryan, and Felice, circa 1987

in our lives. Both boys were athletic, and Ira went to watch them play soccer, baseball and basketball as much as possible. He loved camp visiting days, when the kids got to show the new skills they acquired during the summer.

Bryan played the trumpet, and Adam played the trombone. One time, sitting through an elementary school music performance, I felt myself grimace at a particularly sour note. But when I glanced over at Ira, he had a wide grin on his face. To him, the imperfect music came from the fact that his sons were participating in the performance. That was what mattered to him. That was what moved him.

Unlike so many other families, we always tried to do things together. We took family trips and visits into the city together. We went to museums and ball games. We were always a family.

Carpe diem. That was Ira's motto. Seize the day. He loved being outside, whether skiing, playing paddleball, taking care of the lawn or walking with our dog, Daisy.

We were both from working families, so it never occurred to us that we wouldn't work hard to build the life we wanted for ourselves and our boys. We encouraged and supported one another in our work.

Weekdays were devoted to work, with the weekends devoted to one another and our family. I don't know of any other couple that enjoyed each other's successes—not the "fruits" of those successes,

The Zaslow men at Adam's high school graduation, from left: Bryan, Ira, Adam and Grandpa Hy, Ira's father, June 1996

but the successes themselves—any more than we did. I was proud of everything Ira accomplished, and I was happy knowing that he was proud of me as well.

Our boys grew to be fine young men with independent lives of their own.

Once again, the world lay in wait for Ira and me to conquer together.

And then came September 11th.

The summer of 1965 had been a time of innocence and joy. The summer of 2001 had been even more enjoyable than that. Ira and I had come to a special place in our lives and our relationship. Our time together was as special as it had been during those early days of our "courtship." Only now, it had the added dimension of experience, of a life lived and shared together.

As Ira often said when we considered our sons, "We done good."

We were happy in our accomplishments. We loved our home. We had arrived at a time in our lives when we were financially comfortable enough to think seriously about the various trips and vacations we would enjoy together—now that we were reaching a point in our lives when we would have the time to enjoy them.

Throughout the summer, Ira extended his days by walking with me on the Atlantic Beach boardwalk. We held hands and talked about anything and everything as we moved along. He was mellow and content with life.

And, as for me, I felt a spiritual peace as deep as any I had known throughout my life. We *had* done good. For each other. For our families. For ourselves. And now, we could relax a little more and enjoy our life.

At our friends' party, circa 1996

We took a few day trips over the summer, visiting quaint little towns nearby or going into the city to explore its treasures. In early August, we traveled to Norwich, Connecticut, to enjoy a few days away. I had convinced Ira to stay at a spa where we enjoyed some outdoor activities and massages. The weather was sunny and warm. I can remember lying on a lounge on the grass, watching the clouds go by. Ira always laughed at the formations I saw in those clouds, like hearts or animal shapes. He saw just clouds.

The evenings were spent at either Mohegan Sun or Foxwoods Resort Casino. Ira loved playing blackjack and was pretty good at it. He also knew when to walk away from the table, which I appreciated.

That vacation was relaxing and a great deal of fun.

And then came September 11th.

I have asked myself often, *Why?* Why is my Ira now on the other side of life? Why him? Why did this horrible act of terror take my precious husband along with thousands of others?

As I have always done, I sought to see a meaning in life. I don't believe that anything is arbitrary. This lesson was reinforced for me by a most wonderful lady who came to me during my grieving.

"Think of life as an Oriental rug or as a tapestry. We who are here on earth can only see the rug from underneath. Our perspective does not allow us to see a pattern. Only God and those who have come before us can see the pattern, because they are gazing down at it from above."

I cannot see the pattern. I admit that. I do not pretend to know "why" Ira and the others lost their lives that day. But I have absolute faith that the pattern exists. It is there. Ira was a gift to me and to our family. He was a gift to all who knew him.

If nothing else, Ira and the other souls lost in that attack force us to recall once again that there is too much hatred, too much violence in the world. Yes, there are hateful and hurtful people whom we must confront, but we must also remember that we are all part of the One. We are all children of God, who deserve the chance to live in dignity and peace.

My world seemed whole and secure.

And then came September 11th.

What the world needs now is love, sweet love,
It's the only thing that there's just too little of.
What the world needs now is love, sweet love,
No, not just for some, but for everyone.

Ira would agree.

CHAPTER FOUR

A Lesson from Job

The great Russian writer Fyodor Dostoyevsky once said that in the absence of God, killing is but the falling of a leaf in the forest. In other words, without God, even the most terrible act has no meaning.

And, by the same token, the most brilliant and loving act would have no meaning either.

I have great faith that there is meaning in life. I do not come to this faith by traveling a scholar's path, although I have done a fair amount of reading and studying about spiritual matters. Instead, I come to my faith through the experiences I have had in my life and the certainty that there is a logic, a pattern, that holds all my experiences together. I understand intuitively the image of the tapestry that my dear friend shared with me after September 11th.

Those of us who have enjoyed lives relatively comfortable and without tragedy often find it easy to find meaning in life. Those of us who have suffered often find it more difficult. This is exactly the lesson that is taught in the Bible, in the Book of Job.

In the text, Job is introduced as a prosperous landowner who enjoys the love and affection of a large family. His fields are fruitful, and his livestock is healthy and numerous. He is, according to the text, a man of faith.

We learn, in the early part of the story of Job, that God is well pleased with Job. He is so pleased with him that he presents him to the heavenly host as an example of a righteous man. One of those in the heavenly host is Satan (the first and only time he is introduced in Jewish scripture is in the Book of Job! His "character" here is as a protagonist and *not* as the embodiment of evil).

Satan was not satisfied with God's presentation of Job as such a righteous man. He challenged God by saying that it is easy to be faithful when everything is going your way. "How faithful will Job be if things weren't going so well for him?"

To demonstrate Job's faithfulness, God then tested Job with a series of calamities that few people could endure. Crops failed and still he held his faith. His livestock got sick and still he held his faith. His family died and still he held his faith. He became sick and tormented by pain.

He cried out to God for a sign that his faith was well-placed.

God did not answer.

He cried out again.

And again.

Finally, in a whirlwind, God visited him and demanded, "Where were you when the foundations of the world were laid?"

It seems a strange question in response to a man who had suffered as Job had, but Job was comforted. Why? Because the very existence of God meant that his losses had meaning.

It did *not* mean that those losses were any less painful. Just that, somehow, they were not arbitrary and cruel.

Our faith is never tested by comfort and ease. The meaning of life can rarely be discerned during happy moments. Yet, it is during those times that our souls are braced by the beauty of life to allow us to endure when our faith is tested.

When people stand at Ground Zero and ask, "Where was God?" I wonder if they ask the same question when they witness the beauty of a meadow filled with flowers. Do they ask the same question when they sit and gaze at newlyweds exchange their vows? Do they ask the same question when they hold their first grandchild in their arms?

No. At those times, they don't doubt the presence of beauty and love and meaning. They don't doubt the presence of God.

But God cannot be present at one without being present at the other.

It's just that, like that vast tapestry of life, it is very often difficult to discern from the limited vantage of a single point in time.

Either there is meaning or there isn't.

I believe there is.

Even so, the threads for my own experience of September 11th were already being woven on September 10th. There was just no way I could have understood that at the time.

CHAPTER FIVE

Deepak Chopra and Michael Jordan

There are times when things appear the same on the surface, but just below the surface, everything is changing. September 10th was like that. When the alarm rang, I opened my eyes to another gorgeous morning.

"Rise and shine," I mumbled, shaking Ira gently by the shoulder. Generally he was up earlier than me, but he had said that he'd wanted to sleep a bit later this morning.

"I'm up," he said softly.

"Are you all right?"

"I think I must have eaten something funny yesterday. My stomach is bothering me a little."

I frowned. We often joked about Ira's "cast iron" stomach; a stomachache was an unusual occurrence for him. "Is it bad?"

"No, not bad. It just feels … off. I'll be fine," he added, throwing off the blanket and heading toward the shower.

He seemed fine the rest of the morning, shrugging off my questions about how he felt.

"Maybe it was just a muscle strain," he said. "I feel pretty good now."

I smiled at his empty coffee cup and cereal bowl. "Hasn't affected your appetite," I observed.

He smiled back. "You know how I hate to have anything adversely affect my appetite."

I laughed. That was my Ira.

The morning routine continued without incident. Everyone was awakened. Showers were taken. Meals were eaten. Ira was dressed. I was getting ready.

"I'll speak to you during the day," Ira called up the stairs before he left to get to the train station.

"You'd better hurry or there won't be any more spots," I said. Parking spots near the train station were always difficult to get, and as Ira was taking a later train, I was worried he might not get one.

"No problem," he called back. "Have a good day."

"You, too."

I heard the door close and then the sound of his car starting. I smiled to myself, and I devoted myself to my morning meditation. After I was finished, I turned my attention to what I was going to wear to school that day. Not that the decision was particularly difficult. I always tried to dress comfortably. I also tried to dress simply.

The community where I live, and where I taught, too often values superficial things rather than important things. Nice cars. Nice houses. Clothes. These kinds of messages were constantly being thrust at the middle-school students I taught, and I tried to convey to them in words and deeds that there are things much more important and valuable than how you dress or what kind of car you drive.

My students all came to know the kinds of values I held dear early on in our class time together. They knew I valued my family and loyal friendship. They knew I thought everyone was important. I often told them that "We are a family this year, look out for one another," or "Think about who you are making fun of who might appear different. You don't know who that kid might grow up to be." True to my beliefs about meaning, I presented my subject as an extension of my life and my thoughts.

How else could I bring literature to life? How else could I bring vibrancy to worlds that my students could not otherwise imagine? I brought novels to the classroom that depicted different characters from many backgrounds, like Shirley Temple Wong who immigrated to Brooklyn from China in the 1940s and learned all about

In the classroom, circa 2001

the culture of the times (*The Year of the Boar and Jackie Robinson*) and brilliant Meg and her genius little brother, Charles Wallace, different from the other kids at school, who became time travelers using their scientific knowledge (*A Wrinkle in Time*).

So finding what I was going to wear was not nearly as challenging as it is for some people. But the decision had to be made, and I made it. Five minutes later, I was dressed, my hair was brushed and I was heading for the door myself.

I was fortunate to have a very easy commute. Ira's commute involved a drive to the station to catch his train to take him to Pennsylvania Station in the city and then a subway ride to the World Trade Center. All this, when it went perfectly, took well over an hour. However, he never complained about the commute. As train riders all over the world can attest, there are "train friends" who make the commute enjoyable. Ira often spoke of people he knew from the train—and never saw any other place. He knew the names of their children and grandchildren, when people in the family were sick, when there were weddings, etc. He became friends with Stan, who lived around the corner. Both men discovered that their children, unbeknownst to them, were already friends.

But me, my companionship during my ten- to fifteen-minute drive to work was the radio. Sometimes, I listened to music. More often, I listened to talk radio.

As I pulled up into the parking lot of the school, I was listening to Joan Hamburg interview Deepak Chopra. As I eased my car into my spot, I kept the engine running for just an extra moment or two so I could listen to the end of the interview.

Hamburg had "walked" Deepak through his career before getting to the question of what he was doing that was new.

In response, Deepak described a new meditation he had developed. "Who am I? What do I want?"

The purpose, he said, was simple and straightforward. It was impossible to improve your spiritual self without first having a firm foundation on which to build. "You need to know who you *are*, not who you think you *should* be. That must be the starting point."

And, with that knowledge as the starting point, the answer to the second question becomes the goal, the envisioned "end point."

What do I want?

Who am I?

I thought the exercise was marvelously simple and wise. It just stunned me with its insight. So, when he invited the listeners to the show to try the meditation, I told myself that I would do so the following morning.

Even though I had decided to try the meditation the following day, it occupied my thoughts through much of that day. It even animated some of my conversations with students and colleagues.

"Don't we need to know what we stand for before we can decide what our goals are?" I asked one set of students. To another, I wondered how we set goals for ourselves. To yet another, I questioned how the media created our self-images and made it difficult to determine our sense of self by looking inward.

"I don't think that's true," one of my students challenged.

I smiled. The student was a clear thinker and never accepted anything on face value. I very much enjoyed her participation in all our conversations in class and in the hallways of the school. "What isn't true about it?" I asked.

"Well, I think for myself, and I think most of my friends do, too," she said.

"Okay."

"We think and act in our own way," she went on, growing more certain in her position.

"If that's true, why do so many of you wear the same style clothes, even the very same brand?" I asked the class.

There was a chorus of protest. Everyone in the class sensed their individuality, yet when we did a simple survey, they were surprised to discover that the vast majority of them *were* wearing similar clothes, brands, shoes. Even their hairstyles were similar.

"But what I love is that you all *know* that you are individuals. It's just that you are bombarded by the media into a single sense of what is attractive or what is cool. And that's just for one reason—so someone can sell you something."

I had their attention now. Even though this was a "spur of the moment" conversation, I was convinced it was worthwhile and consistent with the lessons we'd been discussing throughout the beginning of the school year. I sensed my students shift their weight in their chairs and lean forward in a mixture of defensiveness and interest. My words would be listened to carefully. If I was wrong about something, they would let me know—right away! But if what I was saying struck a chord, it would be one of those classes that they would remember for many years.

I was aware of the moment, too. It was for moments like these that I became a teacher. Moments like these are reproduced with alarming frequency on television shows like *Mr. Novak* and *Boston Public,* but the reality in school is very different. Most of our public school education is the result of hard work that is, by varying degrees, enjoyable or difficult.

But this was different.

By definition, transcendent moments are unique. They don't come often. I reveled in the anticipation of this being one such moment.

"Let's just talk about clothes for a minute," I started out. "Even if certain things are fashionable, they don't look good on some people, right?"

My students agreed with the observation. Different body types looked different in different fashions, and fashion choices were sometimes made without being "true" to body type.

"Look at my hair," I then went on, picking up a long lock of my hair. "When I was your age, there was nothing better than long, straight hair." I frowned and they laughed. It was obvious from looking at me that my hair was never "straight." It was wavy, frizzy, curly … you name it. Anything but straight. "I knew girls who would *iron* their hair to make it straight. Can you imagine? Taking a hot iron to their hair to make it straighter—all to look fashionable.

"And the strange thing is, most of those girls were very pretty. And their hair complemented their looks. But they could only see what the fashion *wanted* them to look like, instead of what they really did look like."

I hadn't heard a protest yet. That meant I'd either lost them completely, or they hadn't found anything to argue with yet. Judging from how they were watching and listening so intently, it was clear that I had not lost them.

"Of course, clothes, hairstyles … those things are all superficial. I mean, we place a great deal of importance on them, but what's most important is what's inside," I emphasized.

I received a couple of groans from the class. I had discussed these sorts of things before. I'd even shared with my students my own belief in reincarnation and what I thought I'd been in previous lives—or things I would have loved to have been. I smiled at my "naysayers" and told them I wasn't going to spend a lot of time going over things we'd already discussed. "But you do need to know that people follow fashions in more than superficial things, and if you're going to be happy, really happy, you have to find your own fashion to follow.

"Know who you are and what you want."

Soon after, the bell rang, cutting short our discussion. As it was, the topic was quite heady for middle-school children. They were only just getting to know themselves and, as a result, were anxious *not* to be unique or stand out. And there I was exhorting them to be different.

I only hoped that I was planting a seed that would flower in several more years, when they were young adults in college or even later.

What I found very interesting was how much the simple words of Deepak that I'd heard earlier in the day had animated my conversation with the students. Clearly, he had struck a chord with me.

Knowing my penchant for meditation and spiritual matters, a couple of colleagues who had also heard the radio show in the morning asked me what I'd thought of the interview. They knew I meditated regularly and had even seen me sitting on the Atlantic Beach boardwalk meditating. I was also fascinated by the unseen world and openly talked about it. I shared with them my own reaction and how I had found myself incorporating what Deepak said into my lessons for the day.

They both smiled. They had, too! Clearly there was something profound in the invitation to Deepak's new meditation. As if I hadn't been determined enough, I told myself that I would certainly incorporate the meditation the following morning in my daily meditations.

The remainder of the school day passed uneventfully. It was such a gorgeous day that rather than go directly home, I decided to go over the Atlantic Beach Bridge and walk on the boardwalk there. I can still *feel* the afternoon sun on my face. There were a lot of people on the boardwalk, taking advantage of these last beautiful, summery days before the colder weather started coming in.

As I came up the ramp of the boardwalk and approached the railing, I thought about how envious Ira would be that I was able to come out and enjoy the view of the ocean and the salt air in the afternoon while he was still busy at work.

"That's right," I would sometimes tease him. "I'm off at three o'clock *and* I get all the school holidays, too!"

"Quite the life you've got," he would answer drolly.

Of course, we generally had this discussion when I was up late at night reading and marking students' papers or getting ready for parent-teacher conferences. From the outside, it might appear that teaching is easy and that teachers have a lot more free time than "real" working people, but the fact is, we teachers put in a lot of hours away from school in order to work successfully with young people.

Ira knew that as well as anyone.

Of course, he would still be a bit envious that I would be able to be out on the boardwalk in the afternoon! I thought to myself that if I got back to the house early enough to catch him before he was leaving for his train, I would give him a call just to say hi.

Standing at the railing, I closed my eyes as I faced the sea, and I drew in three deep breaths. Feeling balanced and relaxed, I turned and headed down to the far end of the boardwalk.

Living in the community and teaching at the local middle school, I knew a great many people. I recognized even more by sight. So the walk was often punctuated by greetings and stops for brief conversations. I happened to bump into a colleague who was celebrating her birthday the next day.

"Are you doing anything special?" I asked her.

She waved away the question. "I try not to call too much attention to my birthday anymore."

I laughed along with her. We were both long past finding birthdays exciting.

"We'll probably go out to dinner or something. But it's a 'school night,' so I don't expect much." She shrugged her shoulders. "It's generally a pretty uneventful day when everything's said and done."

"Well, happy birthday," I said, and then I was on my way again. When I finished my "lap" of the boardwalk, I stopped and sat on one of the benches for a moment, just to look at the sky. The sun was sinking, and the sky was streaked with brilliant oranges and flaming reds. The ocean was glittering. The sand looked as soft as down. The air had a coolness to it.

I drew a deep breath.

Who am I? What do I want?

I listened to the radio as I drove back across the bridge toward home. Music. Mostly music from when I was growing up, but there were also some things I liked that were current. Christina Aguilera came on singing "Lady Marmalade" and I danced to the beat in my driver's seat.

I pulled into the driveway and got settled inside. I was preparing dinner when I heard Ira's car pull up.

"Like clockwork," I thought as I glanced at the clock.

Even when the train ran a couple of minutes late, Ira seemed to make up the difference on the way home so that he always arrived at the same time.

"I'm in the kitchen," I called out when the door opened.

He came to the kitchen door and kind of leaned against the door frame. I turned and looked at him. "What's the matter?" I asked. "You look tired."

"I don't know. My stomach started bothering me again."

"Really? When?"

He shrugged. "Middle of the day." Ira looked pale, even with his suntanned skin.

"What did you have for lunch?"

"Just a sandwich. Something light. I don't think it was anything I ate," he added.

"Do you think you're getting sick?"

"I hope not," he said.

Ira hated to be under the weather. He was much too active to be reconciled with the rest that was necessary to get well. He was always the one to go back to work a day or two sooner than he probably should.

"How was your day?" he asked.

"Good. I had a nice walk on the boardwalk," I said.

"Lucky you," he said with a sly smile.

"Are you going to want dinner?"

He thought for a second. "No. Probably not. I think I'll just get out of these things and rest."

When I checked on him, he had changed into sweatpants and a T-shirt and gotten comfortable. He was reading the paper.

"You want me to put the television on?"

He shook his head. "No, I don't feel like the news this evening."

I studied him, worried. It wasn't like him to act that way. Still, his color wasn't too bad. He just looked a little tired. "Maybe you'll stay home tomorrow if you're not feeling well," I suggested.

He glanced at me and raised his eyebrow. "Stay home? Because I have a stomachache? I don't think so. Besides, I'm sure I'll feel better in the morning. It just seems to come and go. I'll get a good night's sleep and that will be that."

I kissed him on the forehead. Ira. My optimist.

I busied myself with some papers from school and with cleaning up. When I checked on him again, he had dozed off. I shook him by the shoulder. "Ira, come on. Get into your pajamas and get cleaned up. Then you can get into bed."

He groaned softly, still asleep, and got up and walked toward our bedroom.

I stopped in by the bathroom door while he was brushing his teeth. "How's your stomach?"

"Better," he said. "A little better."

"That's good."

I watched television downstairs so I wouldn't disturb him. I was watching the news when there was a report that Michael Jordan was returning to professional basketball. Now that was something that Ira would be interested in.

I was still awake when Adam came home.

"Hi, Mom," he said.

"Did you hear?"

"Hear what?"

"Michael Jordan's returning to the NBA."

His eyes widened. "What did Dad say?"

"He doesn't know. He went to sleep early."

"Is he all right?"

I nodded. "He was just tired from a long day."

"I'm going to tell him," he said, already starting to bound up the stairs.

I started to say he shouldn't wake his father, but then I stopped. Ira would probably like Adam waking him up with that news. So, Adam roused his father enough to tell him the news.

"Did you tell him?" I asked Adam when he came back downstairs.

"Yeah, he woke up enough to hear."

"What did he say?"

"He just smiled. I know he was happy. Anyway, I'm getting ready to go to bed. I'll see you tomorrow."

He kissed me on the forehead and went to his room, not knowing that he had just had his last conversation with his father.

I watched the end of the news and then turned off the television. September 10th was over. The next morning, I would try Deepak's meditation, and then it would be a great day.

I was already thinking of some of the ways to continue my discussions from today with my students.

CHAPTER SIX

Last Kiss

How could any of us have known that our faith was about to be tested with a test of Jobian proportions? Before going to sleep that night, the biggest news on television was Michael Jordan returning to the NBA. The news the next night would dwarf that news so mightily as to render it insignificant.

We all went to sleep that night with one understanding of the world. When the morning dawned, we were still innocent, still unaware of the evil that awaited us. Ira had gotten up early, at his usual hour. Even so, he seemed tense and agitated, as though something was occupying his mind.

"Are you all right?" I asked him.

He mumbled his reply. "Yes. Fine."

"Is your stomach still bothering you?"

"A little. It'll be fine."

I was glad to accept his optimistic assessment. One, that was very much like Ira to minimize any negative feelings he might have had; and two, I was anxious to try the Deepak Chopra meditation that I had been thinking about since the previous morning. I think I'd even had a dream about it.

"Well, give me a goodbye kiss now," I said to him.

He looked at me curiously. "I'm not leaving yet. Are you trying to get me to leave?"

I smiled. "No. But I want to try this new meditation."

"Ah, the mystic!" he said affectionately. Then he walked over toward me. I was still standing up when Ira kissed me. Then he rested his head on my chest very lovingly.

It was a lovely sensation, having Ira do that. But even as he did it, I was aware that it was strange. Not because Ira was not affectionate. He was, but rarely in the mornings when he was always in a hurry to make his train.

"Are you sure you're all right?" I asked.

He smiled again, but this smile seemed a bit forced. "Isn't a man allowed to embrace his wife without being held in suspicion?"

"Okay, okay," I joked.

Then I positioned myself in the middle of our bed and crossed my legs and began my meditation.

Who am I? What do I want?

I could feel myself beginning to relax and drift into my meditation when I was disturbed by Ira's arms wrapping themselves around me. Annoyed by being jerked out of my meditation, I squealed, "Hey, what are you doing?" When I opened my eyes, I thought he was just trying to annoy me in his teasing way. But when he kissed my cheek and said goodbye again, I could tell it was a gesture he'd wanted to make. I returned his kiss.

"Have a good day. I'll see you when you get home."

"Maybe we'll go to the boardwalk," he said.

I smiled. "That would be nice. I hope your stomach feels better."

He grimaced. "It doesn't feel better right now," he admitted. "Even the plain toast I had seems to be cramping it up."

I didn't bother suggesting that he stay home. That suggestion would just fall on deaf ears. "Well, see how you feel," I said.

And then he was gone. I returned to my meditation, breathing deeply before focusing on the questions, "Who am I? What do I want?"

Who am I?

I focused on the words as my body relaxed and my consciousness began to loosen. Who am I? A not terribly young anymore—though I still feel it—Jewish woman living on Long Island and teaching in a public middle school. Could that be right? Could that be who I am? The mother of two adult sons. The wife of a man I've loved through most of my life.

Who am I?

I continued to let my thoughts drift as those words came in and out of focus. Suddenly, I was remembering the beach at Beach 23rd Street. I could feel the summer sun heating my young, baby-oiled body. I could almost picture the book I held in my hands. I saw myself looking up and seeing someone come out of the ocean. He was walking toward me.

It was Ira.

"But I'm not sixteen years old anymore," I thought to myself.

I heard the music from the transistor playing. "What the world needs now is love, sweet love..." and I suddenly remembered *how* that young girl thought. I could feel the same feelings she felt when she looked out at the ocean. I felt the same longing she felt when she thought about poetry and the world.

That's who I am, I realized. Still, after all these years. I was an idealistic person who believes in wonderful things. I was a person to whom great things happen. Not earth-shattering things, but simple things that I knew were great. I am a person who appreciates what she has.

That's who I was.

What do I want?

My mind drifted over so many things. In my mind, I revisited the apartment where I grew up, entering the living room where the plastic-covered sofa was, the bedroom I shared with my sister, the kitchen table where I shared meals with my family until the night before my wedding. And my grandparents' apartment, the aroma of my grandmother's delicious soup in the air. Then I visited the rooms of my house. I saw my sons as babies, as toddlers, as young men and as young adults, and experienced the love I felt for them at every stage of their lives. I returned to my bedroom, the room I had shared with Ira for so many years.

And I felt such happiness.

I realized that what I wanted was to keep feeling that happiness. I wanted to continue watching my sons grow and succeed at those things they sought to do. I wanted to see them enjoy their families as much as I have enjoyed mine. I wanted to grow old with Ira.

That was what I wanted: to grow old with Ira.

Then, as if rising up from the deep end of a swimming pool, I "resurfaced" and opened my eyes. I felt refreshed and very "centered." I was comfortable with who I was, and I was happy with what I wanted. I said a silent prayer that everyone could know the same sense of balance and could enjoy the same kinds of joys I did.

I finished getting ready, and then I headed to my car to start my day.

The morning seemed to echo the warmth in my soul. It was a perfectly beautiful September morning. Warm and clear. The sky was a brilliant blue. The air was fresh and clean. Perfect.

I had already decided in my mind to use the meditation again in my classes, to ask my students about various characters we'd read about if they could answer those questions for the characters. And then, maybe, if there was time, I would gently move the conversation back to a deeper introspection on the part of the students.

I knew, from having worked with youngsters for so many years, that such introspection could be very beneficial, although it could be difficult as well. Too many of the students I'd taught came from homes and situations that were not loving. And revisiting those kinds of feelings is troubling. But it was also an opportunity. As Deepak would say, it would be impossible for those kids to get past that without first coming to terms with it.

Reality. What is. That's the starting point.

The more I thought about how I might engage my students, the more convinced I was that it would be successful. I could already picture how some of the students might react, who would be anxious to contribute to the class discussion, whom I would have to encourage.

I was smiling as I drove toward the school. I listened to music this morning. I wanted to focus on my hopes for the day's discussions and lessons without the distraction of talk radio.

Pulling into my parking spot, I couldn't have been more positive about how the day was going to be.

As my students shuffled into the first-period class, I could see that I was going to have to invest some of them with my positive energy if the class was going to work. First period is a difficult one. Some of the students are still half asleep. Of course, first period is often more productive than the final period of the day when the students are tired and anxious to leave school. Each point of the day has its strengths and weaknesses. I generally modify my lessons to anticipate them—as well as the makeup of the particular class.

I greeted my first period warmly, moving around and trying to focus their attention and get them ready to learn.

We were beginning a discussion about using a Writer's Notebook when the phone in my classroom rang. Generally, phone interruptions came later in the day. Students were called out. Lunches were brought to school. Notifications were made.

I instructed one of my students to pick up the phone.

"They want you," he told me after speaking into the receiver.

CHAPTER SEVEN

The Dream

Not long ago, I had a recurring dream that stayed with me long after I woke up. In my dream, I was driving in my car. I was on my way to work but I was running late. I don't remember what had caused me to run late that morning, as I'm generally a very punctual person. But, being late, I found myself feeling increased pressure to get to school as soon as possible.

I turned down a street I'd never traveled down before. It seemed odd to me, that I could live in a community for so long and there be a street I'd never traveled down. But I didn't spend time contemplating that irony. I was late. Like the White Rabbit. Late, late for a very important date.

I had only turned down the street because I thought it might allow me to avoid some of the traffic that was slowing my progress. But, having turned onto the street, I found myself drawn to the interesting buildings and shops that lined it on both sides.

The light seemed somehow brighter. More inviting.

I could see people walking along the street, people who I felt I recognized but didn't know well, like the young woman who jogged early in the morning. Some I knew casually, the friendly nanny of the neighbors across the street. Others, I knew of, like the man running for the school board. But they all seemed to be engaged in interesting, earnest activity.

There were others who I did not know at all.

I found myself interested in finding out more about these people and the interesting shops that lined the street. As I drove along, I searched for street signs so I would be able to find this place again. Yet, even as I felt drawn to this new place, this strange place, this interesting place that seemed to have always been so close by and yet hidden from me, I was aware of the need to get to work.

I pulled over and took my cell phone out of my purse and dialed the school's number.

"Main office."

"Yes, this is Felice Zaslow," I said into my cell. "Who is this?"

The woman gave her name, a name I did not recognize. It was curious that I would not recognize the name of a secretary at the school where I'd taught for all these years and yet all the strangers on the street I'd been driving along seemed to be so familiar to me.

"I just wanted to let you know that I would be late this morning. I've..." How could I explain what had happened? How could I explain that my desire to avoid a bit of traffic had taken me along a new street, one that opened a new world to me? "I've been delayed," I told her.

"Well, that's okay," she said. "But you can't be late every morning, dear."

"No, no, of course not," I agreed.

"Goodbye."

"Goodbye," I said to the cell in my hand, even though the connection had already been lost.

That was all I remembered of the dream. Dreams can mean so many things, and I know that it can be dangerous to put too much stock into a particular interpretation of a dream. But this one, I think, has clear meaning to me.

The new street is my new life. It is one that is both inviting and interesting, though still a bit strange and unsettling. This new, unexplored street is there, ready for exploration. Yet I am still rooted in my "old" life. I continue to go to teach at school. I remain rooted in the world that has always been so secure and familiar.

And yet, it is now almost as strange as the new world that opened up before.

At times, I find myself with the unsettled feeling of speaking into a disconnected cell phone.

Goodbye.

CHAPTER EIGHT

The Phone Call

It's strange how all the little things that clue you in to something momentous don't take on form until *after* the fact. All the things that are so significant and telling. All the details. We all so often miss the details of our lives.

I once had a colleague who claimed that it was *only* in retrospect that the details of our lives take on meaning.

"There's too much background noise while it's happening for us to really make sense of it," he said.

I don't know if I agree with him. I do believe that it is possible to find a quiet space within yourself and "step outside" the everyday craziness in order to see what is important. Wasn't that what I was doing on the morning of September 11th when I sat cross-legged on my bed, trying the Deepak Chopra meditation?

Who am I?

What do I want?

Isn't the active process of asking those questions and listening for the answers the way to silence the "noise" and to understand what is important about life?

But I must admit, had I known what was to come that morning, I would have forgone the meditation and devoted more attention to the last time I would see my husband in this world.

Unlike my recent dream, my drive to school that morning was uneventful. As I punched the buttons on the radio, I stopped at one station in time to hear the end of a song I'd known since I was a young girl. *"What the world needs now is love, sweet love…"*

I hummed along to the final notes of the song as I drove along on autopilot, making turn after turn and following my regular route to school. I pulled into the parking lot and eased my car into my parking spot. Just like every other morning.

As I gathered my bag and materials and got ready to climb out of my car, my colleague's car pulled into the spot next to mine. Like clockwork. I greeted her.

"Traffic was terrible today," she said with a sigh.

It amazed me that, while she ran into traffic and I did not, she still pulled into the spot less than twenty seconds after I did, just like she did every morning. It seemed that no matter what the difference in variable—the number of red lights I hit, or the fact that I have to return to my house because I've forgotten something, or any of the million things that could affect her travel time or mine—she still pulls into her spot within twenty seconds after I pull into mine.

In all the years we've been teaching at the school, I would be hard-pressed to think of more than one or two mornings when that wasn't the case.

On that beautiful September morning, the world seemed that stable and that orderly.

As always, I went into the main office and signed in. The room was a beehive of activity. All the teachers were coming and going, signing in, checking mailboxes, picking up phone messages. One teacher was showing off photographs of her new grandchild. Another teacher was talking about her upcoming wedding. Still another was talking about his son's performance in the previous day's soccer game.

I gazed upon this scene and remembered my morning's meditation. Part of me felt that everything was right with the world and that I didn't want anything more than this. After all, how many times had these same kinds of discussions taken place? How many times had my friends and colleagues taken an interest in my own sons' basketball and baseball games? Hadn't I shown off Bar Mitzvah photographs? And wedding photographs? Hadn't I celebrated by bringing in platters of cookies after such special events? We were a work family, sometimes knowing more about one another's lives than our blood families.

"Good morning, Felice."

I turned and greeted my friend.

"Good morning." "What are your plans after school?" "How was your vacation?" "How's Ira?" "How are the boys?"

As teachers, we take full advantage of the few moments we have together. After all, the rest of our day is spent with our students, and with our students it is their lives and needs that occupy our attention.

Dr. Kavarsky, the school principal, was outside greeting students. I had waved to him as I pulled into the parking lot. Inside, the assistant principals were starting to usher the teachers along to the classrooms, reminding us that the bell would be ringing in a couple of minutes.

We started streaming out of the main office and to our classrooms. There were assignments to write on the chalkboards, materials to prepare and graded assignments and tests to return. All this had to be ready at the beginning of the day. There wasn't much time between classes to get organized for the next period. Not when you had to keep half an ear on the hallways to make sure the students were moving along properly.

The passing bell rang. A moment later, my students began to enter the classroom. One at a time. Two or three together. Some crowding others out.

"Good morning."

I couldn't help but smile as my students came into the classroom. Some of them were cheerful, greeting me and their classmates warmly. Some looked half asleep. Some looked as though they were carrying burdens that no ten- or eleven-year-old should have to carry. Most were just boisterous and talkative, whispering to a friend or slapping a back with "hey, bro."

Every one of them was exceptional in his or her own way. Although the semester was still young, I was looking forward to getting to know my students and seeing them mature over the course of the time we would be together.

As a teacher, I tried to share myself with my students—my feelings, hopes and beliefs. I thought teachers did a disservice to their students by removing who we really were from our teaching. I considered myself more than a "knowledge dispenser." I believed I was a person who had the best chance of positively affecting my students' lives if I could develop an appropriate relationship with them.

As a result, my students know my feelings about karma and my belief in people's essential goodness. They know why I love the stories I love and why I care so much about teaching.

I think those things matter to my students.

The class bell rang. One or two students rushed into their seats after the bell. I gave them my "questioning" look and was rewarded with sheepish shrugs. I decided not to pursue the matter. Not today. It was a beautiful day.

And there was so much to cover.

I was listening to a student's response to a passage in the book we were reading when the classroom phone rang. I asked another student to pick it up. He went to the phone and answered it. He listened for a second and then looked at me.

"They want you."

I hated disturbances like this in class. It was most likely some administrative issue that had to be taken care of. I didn't mind the paperwork, but it annoyed me when it took away from my teaching time. "Excuse me," I said. Then I hurried to where the phone was mounted by the door.

"Yes?"

"Felice, could you come to the main office? There's a phone call for you."

"Is everything all right?" I asked. It was very unusual to be called out of class for a personal call.

"Your son's on the phone."

"I'll be right there."

I apologized to my class, telling them that I had to run down to the main office for a moment. It wasn't until later that I realized they had grown very quiet. I guess the look on my face scared them. It was obvious that I was worried by the request.

I poked my head into the classroom next door and asked the teacher to please keep half an eye on my class. "I have to run down to the office."

Although it didn't make much impression on me at the time, the main office was filled with people, more people than had been there when I arrived that morning. In fact, it was so crowded that I had to ease my way through all the people to get to the counter.

"Felice, around here," the secretary directed me, getting up to guide me around the counter and to the phone.

I sat down at the desk. "Which line?"

"Line two."

I punched the button and picked up the phone. "Hello?"

A second later, I heard the voice of my eldest son, Bryan, on the other end of the line.

"Mom…"

"Bryan, what's the matter? Are you all right?"

"I'm fine, Mom. But a plane just hit one of the towers of the Trade Center. I saw it!"

"What?" I could hear a range of emotions in his voice. There was fear. Disbelief. The kind of tension people feel when they are witnessing something monumental and devastating.

"From the ferry. I'm on my way to Jersey. I saw it, Mom. A plane hit the Towers."

I remembered then that Bryan had been going to New Jersey that morning for a call-back interview at UBS PaineWebber. Ira had known about the interview and was very excited for Bryan. The two of them had discussed how Bryan should "prep" for the interview.

Bryan's next comment focused me. "Lori is trying to reach Dad."

Lori, my daughter-in-law, had been trying to reach Ira since word first came out that the Towers had been hit. She had not yet been successful, although she had left several messages.

I drew a deep breath to calm myself. Bryan was still on his way to his interview and I wanted him to do well. "Okay, well, don't worry. I'm sure everything will be all right.

"Call me back when you hear something."

"Okay, Mom."

"Goodbye," I said, but the phone had already disconnected.

I sat at the desk. I was vaguely aware of all the noise and the hubbub going on around me, but I felt as if I was in a small pocket of quiet. As soon as I set the phone's receiver in the cradle, I felt a powerful sense of helplessness.

I drew another slow, cleansing breath. I searched my mind for something to cling to, something that would calm me. I remembered my mother's words, "No news is good news," and I tried to smile to myself.

"You okay, Felice?"

I looked up at the secretary. I nodded. "Yes, I think so."

I could see that her eyes were worried, but she didn't ask anything else. I felt like a sleepwalker as I wandered in the main office. People were coming in and out, making phone calls, hugging one another, crying. There was talking, but I couldn't discern about what.

I still had no real appreciation of the extent of what had happened. All I had were Bryan's words over the telephone. A plane had hit one of the Towers. In my mind, I was thinking of a small plane.

What else could it have been?

The secretary invited me to go through the door to the principal's office to sit down.

It was only when I stood in front of the television that had been turned on that the reality of what had happened began to sink in. As I stood and watched the image of the black smoke pouring out of the Towers, the cameras shifted to the horrific image of the South Tower beginning its collapse.

There were people running. People crying.

The explosion of smoke that poured down the streets of New York City was unimaginable. How many times had I walked along those very streets?

What was happening?

There was the terrible feeling that the world was coming to an end.

CHAPTER NINE

Waiting for News

Although physicists might claim that time is a constant, I know that they are wrong. All time does not move at the same rate. In the main office of my school, time had slowed almost to the point of stopping still.

I was a sleepwalker. I was surrounded by people I had known for ten, fifteen years, and yet they all seemed slightly unfamiliar. Like people I *thought* I might have met someplace. Their voices were spongy. There were no sharp edges to their words.

The only image that stayed in sharp focus was Ira.

I saw the South Tower come down. I saw the second plane hit. I saw the North Tower come down.

I didn't think that people who had never been to New York City could appreciate the immensity of the World Trade Center. Every modest city now has "skyscrapers"—tall buildings of ten, fifteen, even twenty stories that dominate their cityscape. But the World Trade Center dwarfed *all* those. There were banks of elevators in the World Trade Center that didn't even stop until the seventieth floor.

The World Trade Center rose more than one hundred stories into the air. At any given time, there were over fifty thousand people—workers, travelers, tourists, shoppers—in the Trade Center. Fifty thousand people. That's a small city.

Actually, it's not that small a city.

I had looked out the broad plate glass of Windows on the World, the restaurant on the top of the Trade Center. From there, the Statue of Liberty looked like a toy. Helicopters and small planes regularly flew *below* your feet.

How could anyone who had never been there imagine what that was like, to stand inside a building while helicopters flew below you?

But more than that, the World Trade Center was where Ira worked. It was where he felt comfortable. Like many of his friends and colleagues, he felt the power of the place—"like the heartbeat of the world."

Since the first attack on the Trade Center, in 1993, no one had taken its security for granted. Ira had become a captain for emergency evacuation drills. That thought comforted me. He would find a way out. He would find a way to be safe, all the while helping others along the way.

Meanwhile, all around me, bits and pieces of my colleagues' conversations pierced my dream state. They were finally getting through to their loved ones with news that they were safe.

So where was Ira?

It was unlike him not to call. He would have known how worried we'd all be. He'd have borrowed someone's cell phone if he had to. He would have found a way to get word to me.

The more I thought about that, the more anxious I became. Suddenly, my legs felt rubbery. I eased myself into a chair.

I didn't see my team teacher, Debbie, until she had knelt down at my feet. I looked down at her. I tried to smile. "I'm too young to be a widow," I said, surprised by the words that came out of my mouth.

Without thought, I had given voice to the deep fear I refused to acknowledge—Ira might be dead.

Debbie didn't say anything. She just continued to watch me and hold my hand.

My eyes began to sting. "My life sucks," I said.

"Right now it does," she acknowledged.

"I can't just sit here," I said, suddenly impatient to do *something*. Anything. So I paced.

"Would you like to come into my office and sit to watch the news as it's updated?" Dr. Kavarsky asked me.

I shrugged. I supposed so. What else could I do? There was a numbing quality to what was happening. I felt both exhausted and enervated.

As I sat in the principal's office, one of the school aides, Florence, brought me some water.

"I'm not thirsty," I said.

"You should have something to drink," she said.

I took the glass and drank the water. As I drank it, I realized that I had been wrong. I was incredibly thirsty. I couldn't believe how soothing the water had been or how good it was to drink.

"Thank you," I told her.

Bryan called again. There still had been no word of Ira. Bryan knew of some of Ira's colleagues, other men and women who had gotten out of the building, but none of them had any word about Ira.

They hadn't seen him.

"I have to go home," I announced.

"Of course," Dr. Kavarsky said. He asked if I needed anyone to go with me. I told him that I didn't. That I was all right.

"You're sure?"

I nodded.

It seemed so strange to be leaving school in the middle of the day, driving along the very same streets I had driven only a few hours earlier. Only now, they seemed foreign and confusing. I would drive for blocks at a time, only to be startled when I realized I had no recollection of having driven the past few blocks.

"Concentrate, Felice," I told myself.

I listened to the radio, hoping to hear some music, but all the stations were playing the same thing: the news. Lost in the destruction of the Towers was any thought of the world needing love.

My younger son, Adam, was already home when I got there. He came out to meet me at my car. He had been on his way out to find me.

"Find me?"

"I called the school. They said you'd left to come home, but that was a long time ago."

Had the drive home taken that much longer than it usually did?

"I'm sorry if I worried you," I told him.

I could see in his expression that not knowing where both his parents were was a very big strain.

"Dad will get out," he said.

"I know," I told him. "I know."

Time continued its uneven pace. Minutes were like hours and then, suddenly and unexpectedly, I realized that hours had flown by in what seemed like minutes. Cathy, a considerate and kind friend of mine for many years, stopped by.

Cathy made sure that I ate something and drank water or juice. It just seemed so unreal to be concerning myself with these trivial, physical needs. My emotional and spiritual world had been turned upside down, and eating or drinking seemed to be the last thing I needed.

"Man does not live by bread alone," right?

Yet, as soon as I ate and drank something, I realized just how famished or thirsty I had become.

And at every instant, I expected to hear from Ira—a phone call from a Long Island Railroad platform telling me that he was just waiting for his train—or maybe the sound of the door opening and him coming home. "What's for dinner?" Just like that.

But that didn't happen. Several of Ira's colleagues called. Like everyone else in the city, they were checking and cross-checking on each other, doing roll calls to make sure everyone was accounted for.

No one had spoken to Ira.

One of Ira's colleagues did say that a young man who worked in the office had said he'd spoken to Ira in the morning.

I anxiously awaited that man's phone call.

And so the minutes and hours ticked by. Another friend, Martha, came over as soon as her teaching was finished for the day. She brought written instructions about how to help families cope with the "waiting period."

"Is that what this is?" I asked her. "A waiting period?"

She nodded.

"What am I waiting for?"

"News," she said simply.

I drew a breath. News. That was all I'd seen all day. News. News. And more news. I'd been bombarded with news. And all the same news. The same images. I wanted, needed, something different.

I needed something that was relevant to me and my life. I needed to hear something about Ira. I needed to hear from Ira.

Waiting.

"I've never been so actively doing nothing before in my life," I told her.

She nodded.

An hour or so after Martha arrived, her husband joined us. Jesse took charge, organizing friends to man the phones and do anything else that needed to be done. There was so much activity going on around me, and nothing was getting done.

I happened to glance at the clock. Eleven o'clock at night. I felt my stomach knot. Eleven o'clock and my precious husband still wasn't home.

"You should try and get some sleep," Martha told me.

Martha and Jesse stayed over that night.

Adam, my grown son, lay down on my bed. I don't know if he slept, but I fell into a dreamless sleep. When I awoke the following morning, I didn't feel any more rested than I had when I'd laid my head down the night before.

CHAPTER TEN

No Stone Unturned

Growing up, my friends were mostly Jewish. I did have a few Catholic friends and I remember having discussions with them about heaven and hell, God, good and evil. When it came to the Catholic view of the afterlife, I understood the way my friend described it—except when it came to the status of babies who died before they'd been baptized. According to my friend, their souls were in limbo.

"Limbo?"

My friend nodded. "Kind of in-between. No place really."

The idea of limbo disturbed me. However, my sense of limbo was only intellectual until the morning of September 12, 2001. From the time I woke up on that morning, and for the following few mornings, I understood only too well what it meant to be caught in spiritual, psychological and psychic limbo.

There were moments of hope, of expectation when the phone rang, only to find I was still waiting.

I had fallen asleep the night before only because I was too exhausted to stay awake. There was no restfulness in my slumber. No dreams. No sanctuary. My sleep was a physical necessity, no different than eating and drinking. I took no pleasure in any of these activities.

In fact, every time I had something to eat or drink, I felt as though I were watching myself eating and drinking, curious to discover that my body needed something that I had so little desire for. There were times during the day when I felt like I was observing myself, that I was like an actor in some horrible drama.

But it was really me, and it was not simply a drama—it was my life.

I woke early in the morning. The house was quiet but unsettled. Adam was still sleeping. His presence convinced me that the preceding day had really happened; it wasn't just some bad dream. I slipped out of the bedroom without waking him. I splashed my face with cold water and looked at myself in the mirror.

The face was familiar, but somehow I didn't look like myself. I had changed. My eyes seemed older. My expression more worried.

"Enough, Felice," I told myself. "There's things to do!"

And there were. Many things. I was determined that this was the day when I would find my husband, alive and well.

I was in the kitchen when the phone rang.

"Hello."

"Hi, Mom."

"Hi, Bryan, how are you doing?"

"I got a little sleep," he conceded, although I could tell by his voice that he didn't get much, and what he had gotten hadn't eased his exhaustion.

"Me, too," I told him.

"Adam is still asleep?"

I glanced back in the direction of my bedroom. "Yes, I think so. He was a few minutes ago."

"I went to the Armory," he said.

I didn't yet know that the Armory had been set up as the repository of information for missing people from the Trade Center. I was soon to learn a great many things that I hadn't known before.

"What's at the Armory?" I asked him.

He described the family center that had been set up. It seemed to be a central area where people hurt or displaced by the tragedy would know to go to be reunited with their families, similar to the centers set up in Europe after the Second World War. What I didn't understand yet was that for the people who hadn't been located during the first few hours, there would be precious few happy reunions.

Precious few.

"I need some things of Dad's," Bryan said.

The request confused me. What could he need of his father's, until his father was located? "What sort of things?" I asked him.

"I don't know. His hairbrush. Eyeglasses. Maybe his toothbrush." Bryan's voice caught as he mentioned each of these items.

"They need anything that might have Dad's DNA on it," he went on.

I felt my heart racing and then getting caught in my throat. I tried to breathe through the panic that was rising inside me. "Okay," I said softly. "How shall I get them to you?"

"I don't know," he admitted. "I guess just gather the things for now. Mom?" he said after a pause.

"Yes, Bryan?"

"Maybe you should call the dentist and see if you can get Dad's dental records."

I didn't say anything.

"Mom?"

"I'm here, Bryan," I told him, blinking away the stinging in my eyes.

"Do you want me to call him?"

I shook my head. "No, I'll take care of that," I told him.

"Okay."

"How are you holding up?" I asked him.

"I'm tired," he admitted. "But I know we'll find Dad."

"Me, too."

A little while later, Dr. Scheer, our internist, called to see if there was anything he could do. Clearly, the word had gone out that Ira was unaccounted for. From what I understand, during those first few hours, people all over the world were checking in with anyone they knew who might have been in New York during the attack.

Given the size of the Towers and the numbers of people who were regularly in them, the number of people who weren't accounted for was amazingly small. But if your loved one was among them, there was no larger group in the world.

Emotionally, the day was a roller coaster. The house was filled with a constant stream of visitors. The phone was ringing off the hook. People delivered food. People urged me to eat. People asked what they could do for me.

"Find Ira," I would say.

I heard from the New York Police Department that there was a real possibility that there were people underground in the PATH train station.

"Really?"

"Yes, we think that an underground cavern might have been formed."

They were grasping at straws, but these were straws I was grateful to consider. The police officer also told me about the handfuls of survivors who were in hospitals around the metropolitan area. People who had been injured and transported to hospitals while unconscious and would most likely recover.

I prayed that one of those poor souls was my husband, my strong, intelligent husband. *Please let him be safe somewhere. Anywhere.*

Most of the injured who had made it to hospitals had been outside the Towers. They had been injured by falling debris or had some other injury. The point was, Ira simply *had* to have gotten out of the Towers.

I had been in frequent contact with my sister, Michele, who lived in Greenwich Village. We agreed that Ira might think to go to her apartment on West 10th Street, a short distance from the World Trade Center. "Maybe he will find his way to your place," I said, trying to reassure us both.

Looking back at those first few hours and days, I can hardly remember how one day blended into the next. There were moments that stood out. Phone calls that seemed to distinguish themselves from the ongoing sameness of hope, fear, dread and desperation.

My family was always surrounded by large numbers of good friends and neighbors during those days. Anything that had to be done was done by dozens of volunteers who wanted only to be able to do *more* for us. The closer the relationship, the more insistent the advice.

"You have to eat, Felice," Marilyn, my dear friend, said.

"I'm not hungry," was my regular response.

"You have to keep your strength up."

I looked at her, imagining how frightening I must have seemed just by the effort to remain cheerful and positive that I could see on her face. "What difference does it make?" I wondered more than once.

"What difference does it make?" she asked rhetorically. "It makes all the difference in the world. You have to be strong for the boys. And for Ira."

I lowered my head. "All right."

Whatever I ate had no taste, but that didn't stop me from eating. My body was famished. It craved sustenance.

There were times when the crowds of people were more irritating than helpful, times when I just wanted to scream at everyone and tell them to leave me and my family alone! I knew that their intentions were so caring and good. But the emotional roller coaster did not leave me much energy to be overly concerned with their feelings.

My focus was too locked in on my boys and Ira.

When I was feeling particularly claustrophobic from all the people in my house, my friends Naomi and Martha did a great job of monitoring the flow of "people traffic." They thanked people for their kindness and explained that I was resting or that I was with someone or that I was having a particularly bad "moment."

Actually, I have no idea what they said to anyone. All I know is that they were the wonderful "gatekeepers" who made sure that I was surrounded by loving and caring friends without being overwhelmed by them.

The sense of unreality that I was feeling could not be overestimated. There had been such a sudden and traumatic breach in the regular flow of my life that it was incomprehensible to me. The fact that the breach had shattered the flow of life for all Americans, and most of the world at the same time, was no comfort to me.

It seemed that the television was always on, and the images were always the same.

The one advantage of being part of *this* tragedy, as opposed to a strictly individual tragedy, was that every agency and person seemed determined to be as helpful as possible.

The reality of what had happened only started to sharpen when all the details of those days—the notepads, the phone calls, the lists—seemed to revolve around the determined efforts of Lehman Brothers, Ira's employer, to do the right thing.

Lehman Brothers called regularly. At first, the phone calls were haphazard. A colleague. A supervisor. A longtime friend. All calling to see if I'd heard anything or if there was anything they could do. Then, the phone calls became more "organized." Lehman Brothers had made all the appropriate contacts, finding out how best to connect the families of their missing employees with grief counselors.

It was clear that there had been a tremendous amount of consideration given to how best to approach those of us who had family members still unaccounted for. They were assessing the needs of the families as best they could.

I don't know how they'd determined the time had come to speak with me regarding a subject that had too much finality for me to think about.

"Mrs. Zaslow, Lehman Brothers has calculated an appropriate benefits package in addition to the one Ira had already established. When you are ready, we will be glad to discuss it with you."

"I'm not ready," I told them directly. "I won't leave a single grain of sand unturned."

The voice on the other end of the line was understanding and reassuring. "We will do everything we can to help."

CHAPTER ELEVEN

Search and Rescue

The police suggested that I check the activity on Ira's ATM card. At first, that seemed to me to be a silly suggestion. What did they think, that Ira was out there somewhere withdrawing cash? But I had promised myself to do anything to find Ira, and so I followed the suggestion.

Lo and behold! There was a record of a transaction on September 14th! I didn't know how to react to this news. Already, I had heard about family members of other missing people who came home to find messages from their loved ones on their phone machines or on their cell phones. These messages filled them with unbelievable hope—but then that hope was dashed when they discovered that the phone calls had been made early on September 11th and that the messages had been lost in the phone system, only surfacing two, three, even four days later.

However, as much as my "rational" self was determined to keep this news in context, my emotions were completely in an upheaval. September 14th! Didn't that prove that Ira had survived the Towers?

I couldn't believe it. In my mind, I pictured Ira wandering around the streets of New York, suffering from amnesia. Then I had an image come into my imagination that caused me to smile. Ira was a very good-looking man, and I had the image of some woman spotting him and, rather than making sure he got home to his family, deciding she would keep him for herself!

I pictured him having dinner at this woman's apartment when he finally came back to himself and realized that he had to get home.

"Shit!" I heard him say to himself, "I'd better call Felice!"

I couldn't help but laugh out loud as that image played out in my mind. But when someone asked me what was so funny, I simply answered, "Nothing. Nothing. I was just thinking of something someone said a long time ago."

The discovery of the transaction made a lot of other people hopeful, as well. Lehman Brothers was going to great efforts to discover everything they could about the employees still missing. They were searching for the last people to see them. But with this information, they redoubled their efforts to find Ira.

They hired the Beau Dietl detective agency to trace Ira's whereabouts on the morning of the 11th. They searched for everyone who might have seen Ira as well as checked the area hospitals to see if he might have been taken there and remained unidentified.

With the detective agency involved, I became more hopeful. *They* would find my Ira. I was certain of it. I felt that maybe there was some added momentum behind our search, and I wanted to do everything I could to aid that momentum.

I was aware of the news that was being broadcast over and over and over on television and radio. Everyone was. We all knew that the odds of any survivors were diminishing with every passing hour and day. However, there were also incredibly hopeful signs.

Word that the underground PATH station could have remained relatively unscathed, and that therefore tens or even hundreds of survivors could have been in the air pocket created by the station, raised incredible hope.

I could picture my Ira, leaving some money on the counter when he took something to eat from one of the deli or newspaper stands that were in the station—stocked with pastries, cookies, sandwiches and sodas.

If only Ira could have made his way down to the PATH station, I thought. We would find him there.

I called the rabbi of our synagogue, asking for help. "Surely someone in the congregation knows someone who could help expedite the search," I noted.

We all knew someone who knew someone who knew someone. Isn't that the lesson of the "six degrees of separation"? Surely I would be able to find someone who could get the search for Ira on "high priority" and find him. But I learned that, although there were many, many people anxious to help, they were already doing everything they could. All the resources available were already at work to find survivors.

Didn't they know that time was of the essence?

Of course they did. And their awareness of the urgency of their task was communicated to me every time I tried to push the case. Everyone, and I do mean everyone, did everything they could to assure me that they would do what they could to find Ira.

And I believed them.

Meanwhile, the phone never stopped. Either I was making a phone call or receiving one. I began to think of the phone as some kind of cosmic umbilicus that was keeping me connected to everything and everyone around me. As much as I was emotionally overwrought by the waiting, I was hardly the only one. Not only were my two sons as fully involved as I was, so was Ira's father, Hy.

Since Hy had moved to Florida, joining the ranks of Jewish retirees to the sun-drenched state, we had never considered him to be particularly far away. We visited when we could, hopping on a plane for the short flight. So many people were involved in the New York–Florida axis that there were many times Florida seemed like an outer borough of New York City. However, with the devastation of the Twin Towers, Ira's father felt far, far away.

The telephone was our best connection to avoid despair. All he had to go on were the horrible images that were being broadcast night and day over the television.

"How could anyone have survived that?" he asked over the phone, his voice filled with anguish.

Although it seemed inconceivable, the truth was that thousands and thousands had. The earlier terrorist attack in 1993 had taught the occupants of the buildings valuable lessons. Evacuation plans were devised and put into place. People knew where to find staircases.

There was a great deal of reason to hope.

"Did you see them? They were jumping from the windows!"

Those images were among the most devastating of the attack. That people would leap from seventy flights up was inconceivable. Yet they did. What horror must have been behind them that they opted for that? Even now, I shudder at the thought.

But even in those horrible images, I found hope for Ira. Only those floors most directly affected by the airliners seemed to have been completely devastated. Others had time to get out.

And people in the second Tower, if they had reacted to the attack, had more than enough time to get out of the building.

Yes, there were confused messages. Were people to go downstairs to the street or upstairs to the roof? Were they to stay put in their offices or evacuate? How could there not have been some confusion? Even with the best plans in place, the disorientation that must have followed immediately after the plane hit must have taken a little time to get over.

But thousands and thousands *did* get over that disorientation. They got out of the Towers. They were out on the streets before the Towers began to collapse.

"Ira will be all right," I reassured his father. "You have to believe that."

It was easy for me to tell him that. I still believed it myself.

The house was a constant beehive of visitors and activity. Friends and relatives visited constantly, both to offer support and to allay their own worries and fears. One night, while surrounded by so many people whom I loved and who loved Ira, I got everyone's attention.

"Could I have your attention for a minute?" I asked.

Conversation quickly stopped and all eyes turned to me, standing by the couch in my living room.

"Thank you all for being here. You know how important you are to Ira and me. With all your love, I know we can help Ira …"

With that, I asked everyone to gather in the living room and form a healing circle. When everyone had come into the living room, we held hands and, with our eyes closed, one by one we uttered our prayers and love for Ira.

"Please give Ira the strength to survive this ordeal," I prayed. "Wherever he is."

That was my concern, that Ira stay strong—physically, mentally and spiritually. In my mind, there was no doubt that he was alive. But I needed him to be able to *remain* alive until help could get to him and bring him home.

I refused to allow any kind of negativity in the house, or around me for that matter. I just refused to put up with it. So, when one guest arrived with a cake, I reacted harshly.

"You shouldn't have brought a cake," I told her. "I'm not sitting *shiva,* you know!"

I think she was stunned by my reaction. In her mind, she was only being considerate, not wanting to come to the house "empty-handed." But in my mind, her gesture was too closely associated with a house of mourning, and I would have absolutely none of it.

I wouldn't allow the cake into the house.

Chastised, she took the cake back out to her car and then she came back in, apologizing for upsetting me.

"You didn't upset me," I assured her. "I just can't have that kind of karma in the house. Not now. I hope you understand."

She smiled and said that of course she did, but I don't know that she did. Not that it mattered. Most of our lives, we are balancing the needs of everyone around us with our own needs. We compromise. We extend ourselves. However, there are times when we just have to say, "This is how it must be."

The days after September 11th were days when the needs of me and my family took precedence over just about everything. Thankfully, almost all of our friends and neighbors not only understood that, they embraced our needs as their own and helped us through those difficult days.

Healing circles and positive prayer came to be the hallmarks of our house during those hours and days. I would not allow doubt to seep in. Wherever Ira was, whatever condition he was in, it didn't matter. I wanted the spiritual help that we could send him to be perfect. I wanted our energy to get to Ira and to comfort him and to make him strong.

I had no doubt that the energy that was sent out from our home during those hours found its way to Ira and soothed his soul and his body. That was my most deeply held desire. Second to that was that the energy would give him the strength to find his way back home to us.

Regardless of my efforts, difficult and foreboding news did trickle in. We learned that the ATM transaction that had been made on Ira's card, the one that gave me such hope, despite being dated September 14th, had turned out to be an error in the processing of the card's transactions.

A "computer glitch," they'd called it. A mistake. Something to do with the transfer of European American Bank to Citibank.

To me, it was a dark cloud. Still small. Still on the horizon. But ominous. Some of the sun was starting to be blocked for me.

CHAPTER TWELVE

Did I Miss Anything?

Looking around my house on the morning of September 13th, I was suddenly taken with a powerful "nesting instinct." Or maybe, I just couldn't stand the mess. Ira and I always lived very busy lives. Between all the things we did, our sons did, his work, my school papers scattered on the table, our house always bore the signs of movement and energy.

There were always things going on. Basketballs by the front door, sneakers or baseball cleats by the closet, gym shorts on the floor in front of the hamper rather than *in* the hamper. Coats and jackets draped over stairway railings rather than being hung up in closets. Books—always books—on tabletops, on steps, beside the bed.

But, despite this "hubbub" of activity, there was a calm center, a fundamental "neatness" in our house. Dishes were never left in the sink. Clothes didn't get left in stacks. Food was wrapped and put away.

With all the people coming and going, caring and helping, there was no lack of hands willing to take care of cooking and cleaning. But somehow it wasn't *my* house and my life when I had so much help. Little things were out of place. Dishes weren't put in the dishwasher the same way I'd have put them in. Laundry was done, but not folded a certain way.

I don't think I could have made it through the first couple of days without all my friends and neighbors reaching out and helping to do the mundane things that have to be done around a house. I probably wouldn't have eaten anything without prompting.

But, when I woke up on the 13th and looked around, I knew I had to do something that would make my house feel completely like mine and Ira's again. But what?

With my motherly nesting instincts in gear, I decided to put some laundry away. However, when I brought the laundry to our bedroom, I couldn't bear to open Ira's drawer. I just looked at it and stopped.

I might have tried to overcome my emotions and made myself put the laundry away, but I try to be sensitive to those things that are deeper than emotions. I knew that there was a reason that I wasn't to put Ira's laundry away just yet. So the laundry remained in the basket, and despite my emotion, I was somewhat pacified that I had touched on something deeper.

The next morning, when I woke up, I looked at the laundry basket. Then I looked at the drawer. Okay. The laundry would be put away.

I opened Ira's drawer and, tucked behind the drawer face, a greeting card popped up to greet me.

Ira had always been in the habit of saving greeting cards. Whether from our sons or from me, or even the cards he'd sent us, they all seemed to find a way to be saved and tucked away in a safe place. So it wasn't terribly unusual to discover an errant greeting card in Ira's drawer.

I reached for this one and began to read it.

I miss your face,
  I miss your laugh,
  I miss your smile,
    I miss your jokes,
I miss your conversation,
I miss your deep thoughts,
I miss your silliness,
  I miss your wit, I miss your eyes, I miss your nose, I miss your company, I miss your attitude, I miss your advice. I miss yourself.

My hand was shaking as I opened the card. Inside, it went on to say:

Dear Felice,
Did I miss anything?
I love you forever.
IZ

Tears were streaming down my cheeks as I looked at the date of the card:

9/14/98

I couldn't have opened Ira's drawer to find it the day before. That would have been September 13th. I was meant to find this on the third anniversary of when it was sent.

I held the card against my chest and felt my heart beating through the paper. What did it mean? Was Ira trying to tell me something?

Was he communicating to me that he was still alive? Or that he had passed on?

I didn't know, but at least he was communicating, and that gave me some comfort.

CHAPTER THIRTEEN

Acceptance

I still believed that Ira was alive. Until I could be shown otherwise, I would continue to believe that. He was out there somewhere. We only had to find him.

A neighbor had called later that morning and expressed her condolences to me with the message, "Life really sucks sometimes."

I listened to the message and, after taking the measure of my neighbor's voice, I picked up the phone and called her back. "You're right," I told her. "Life does sometimes suck. But even though this is a difficult time, I haven't given up hope yet."

I could tell in her voice that, even though *I* had not given up hope, she was one of the ones who had decided that whatever glimmer of hope had been there in the first day or two was rapidly vanishing. "If there's anything I can do," she said.

"Thank you," I told her. "Just pray for Ira's continued strength," I told her. "Remember, there's a lot of hope that people will be found in the PATH station."

I had begun to envision that underground station as something of a sanctuary, a holy place. It was there that I pictured the missing people gathering and awaiting rescue. It was to that physical place that I often directed my prayers and thoughts, trying to send that positive energy and love so it would most quickly find Ira.

But, as the hours and days continued to go on, I found it harder and harder to maintain hope.

I had always been a spiritual person and an optimist. While I knew that people who were distanced from the spiritual world find any meaningful talk of spiritual things a bit foolish, I had never been a fool. I was a romantic, but not a hopeless romantic. I believed in people's goodness, but I certainly could acknowledge that many people are not good.

I continued to hope for Ira's safe return, but I was not ignorant of how all the signs were moving away from my ever seeing or holding Ira again. Each day became more and more difficult to hold out hope for a happy reunion. The word "miracle" was used more and more in our house.

Finally, when even I could not put it off any longer, I arranged a meeting with the people from Lehman Brothers and the detective who had been in charge of the search. Knowing I could never have that meeting without support, I also asked Adam to be there. Along with the two of us, our rabbi, Rabbi Alan Lavin, and my friend Howie, Marilyn's husband, were at the meeting.

How odd that meeting was! How surreal! These people came to my house, and I greeted them as I would any other guest. "Can I get you anything to drink?"

I put out some small cakes and cookies, and I made coffee. Participating fully in this strange drama, my guests indicated how they liked their coffee. They took small plates and put a cookie or two on them.

Then we settled down at the table.

Just like it was any other sensible meeting.

But this was not any other "sensible" meeting or visit. This was like...I didn't know. All I knew was that I felt a sense of dread each time one of them began to speak. The detective had a manila folder that filled me with fear.

"Well, then," he said, after sipping some coffee. "I was able to find out a fair amount about your husband..." he began as he opened the folder.

I listened, but it was as if his words were coming from far away. He showed us the evidence he'd gathered about Ira's whereabouts on the morning of the 11th.

"As you can see," he went on, pushing some papers onto the table, "your husband sent some emails between 8:29 and 8:31." He showed us copies of the emails Ira had sent during those couple of minutes. They were just quick responses to a couple of emails he'd received and a couple of others to contact colleagues.

"He must have left his computer and desk just after the last email he sent," the detective said. "According to his colleagues…"

"You've spoken with people who saw Ira that morning?"

He nodded. "Yes. Everyone I could find who might have had any contact with Ira that morning. Based on everything I've learned, it seems that your husband went to the Sky Cafeteria shortly after leaving his desk."

I closed my eyes. That was just like Ira, to go to the Sky Cafeteria. He loved being up there. He enjoyed talking to the people who worked up there, as well as the people he met there. "They're like train friends," he told me once. Besides, he'd always said that they had the best muffins in the world.

The Sky Cafeteria was located on the forty-third floor of the North Tower. Based on what the detective was able to deduce, Ira would have been in the elevator on his way back down from the cafeteria when the plane hit.

One of the very worst places to be.

Why hadn't he just stayed in his office and had breakfast there? Why couldn't he have spent *that particular morning* with his friends and colleagues from work?

But wasn't that just like Ira, to go and eat what he wanted when he wanted?

It was after listening to the detective that I felt, for the very first time, that there was no hope of finding Ira alive. The elevator! My God, the terror must have been beyond belief.

I don't remember much more about the discussion—if discussion is the right word for what went on that evening. Someone, maybe the rabbi, questioned the detective about how accurate the information he'd received was.

"We've found that, in this instance, the recollections of colleagues and friends have been very consistent and accurate. I'm sorry to say."

Rabbi Lavin and Howie remained after the others had left. They hovered near me, wanting to do whatever was best for me.

I felt so exhausted after they'd left that I just eased back onto the couch in my living room. "I need an angel," I said out loud. "I really need an angel."

Not two minutes later, the phone rang. I reached for it and picked it up.

"Hello?"

"Mrs. Zaslow?"

"Yes."

"This is Rabbi Kaminetsky. Your husband was a good man. I met him at Temple Hillel. He was active in the Men's Club..."

"My husband wasn't involved in the Men's Club," I said, confused by the phone call. Even if Ira had wanted to be involved in such activities, his long hours at work didn't allow for much. Besides, Ira ate pizza and played paddleball on Saturdays. Hardly the "M.O." of an active Men's Club member.

"Well, he was a good man, and he is now before God in heaven. Do not worry, he is being rewarded for his good works here on earth."

I might not have believed the Men's Club connection, but I certainly believed what the rabbi had just said.

"He has left behind a beautiful woman and two sons who will always give him *nachas* (pride and joy) in heaven. He will see his grandchildren from heaven."

I found great comfort in the rabbi's words, because I believe that Ira was a good and loving person. He cared deeply about others, and his actions and relationships in life demonstrated his feelings. I believed that Ira's good works would be rewarded.

Rabbi Kaminetsky went on to tell me about his own offspring, several generations of them.

"Where do you find the strength?" I asked him.

"I gain strength by giving strength," he said.

A moment later, I rested the receiver in the cradle.

"Who was that?" Howie asked me.

I looked up at him. "A Rabbi Kaminetsky," I said.

"That man's a mystic," he said. "I've seen him, and he has an other-worldly look in his eyes."

"Well, he called the right woman," I said.

To this day, I don't know how the rabbi got my phone number. All I know is that when I most needed to hear the voice of an angel, he called.

The days continued to march on. With each passing day, the chances of Ira returning to me diminished. Through all this, I joined millions of others in gaining strength from the mayor of New York City, Rudolph Giuliani. Watching him as he led his city during this painful time, I couldn't help but wonder if it wasn't *bashert* (meant to be) that he had dropped his run for the Senate.

I deeply believe that things happen for a reason. Who would have thought that a man considering a run for the United States Senate, thrown off by prostate cancer and its treatment, would have actually been playing a part in a much larger drama?

I'm sure that, at the time, Mayor Giuliani was profoundly disappointed by having to give up on his dream of running for the Senate. And, I'm sure, being diagnosed with cancer was very frightening. However, it was only because of the cancer that he didn't run for the Senate and so remained as mayor of New York City, which is where he needed to be on the morning of September 11th.

He helped lead all of us through some of the darkest days of our lives. His leadership was an inspiration to all of us.

However, even as we moved forward with the "recovery" effort, I was lost in a spiritual limbo. I couldn't bear the thought of not finding Ira. I had begun to come to terms with the reality that he wouldn't be returning home, but I wanted to find him. I couldn't bear to think of him lost in that horrible devastation.

"Please, God," I prayed, "I need to find him and I need to find something of his." Then I spoke directly to Ira. "Ira, I need to find your body. I need to have something of yours."

He would know how I could not begin to rebuild my life until I was able to bury him, so he could truly rest in peace.

CHAPTER FOURTEEN

Getting My Sea Legs

If anyone wants to find a way to begin the process of healing after experiencing a tragedy, he should just work with children. Their resiliency is remarkable.

True to their developmental levels, they quickly tired of the many counseling sessions and memorial discussions that they had been put through. Middle-school children use the term "bored" quite regularly. In this case, more than their boredom, they were communicating their need to have things "get back to normal," going to class and after-school activities, having fun with friends.

The question was, would my being back in the classroom really make things "normal" again? It was a question that I couldn't answer. They didn't know either. What they did know was that they were done with "talking things through" and "telling people what they were feeling."

They just wanted to "be" again.

So, when I returned to my classroom, on a Friday, convinced that I would be able to "ease myself" back into my responsibilities, I met with a large number of students who were very happy to see me but not at all interested in discussing the events of September 11th.

This reaction gave me pause during my first period of teaching. In anticipating returning to school, I had made myself very prepared to have an open chat with any and all of my students. I was ready and willing to share my own feelings about that day and my personal loss.

When the bell rang to start first period, I looked out at a group of students who looked more *alive* than I'd remembered. More full of bustling energy and color.

They also looked just a bit sheepish and uncomfortable, as though they had been forced to go to the house of an aunt they didn't know particularly well.

I smiled at my class and then told them that if there were any questions, any questions at all that they wanted me to respond to, I would be happy to do so.

Their answer was a resounding and unanimous, "No."

I was taken aback but quickly regained my footing. "Okay, then, why don't we look at our text..."

And just like that, I was back in the classroom, doing my job. I was teaching. Teaching young people. I taught and I taught. One period followed another. I taught subjects and books I had been teaching for years. There were times when I glanced at the clock on the wall and realized with some surprise that half an hour had gone by. Just like that.

When I asked my colleagues how I was doing in the classroom, they told me I was doing "amazingly well."

I was back. But back to normal? Hardly. Even the practicalities of my day had been adjusted. The secretaries in the main office had arranged for me to go directly to my classroom instead of following the "sign-in" procedure. My team teachers monitored the flow of people coming to see me during the day.

They were like my gatekeepers, making sure that unwanted guests stayed away so I could just get through each day. More than keeping others away, they made sure that they were always *there*.

The support I received from my team and my other colleagues during that difficult time is something I will remember and cherish for the rest of my life. It was as though I was lifted on their hands and well-wishes.

I remember, long ago, going to a fine restaurant with Ira and being amazed at how efficiently the waiter took care of our every need.

Water glasses were filled before we knew they had to be. Wine, too. Just enough time was given for each course, not a moment too much, not a moment too little.

It was so *relaxing* to be in an environment where my needs were so perfectly anticipated and responded to.

Not to diminish the graciousness of the wait staff at that restaurant, but I think it is probably fairly simple to anticipate when a water glass needs to be filled. It is much more difficult and subtle to anticipate a person's emotional needs and to respond perfectly and adequately to them. But during those first days when I returned to my school, that is exactly what my team did for me.

That ability to do so was partially the result of the many hours we'd worked together over the years. In addition, my team teachers had visited me at my house and had spoken to me many times since the terrorist attack.

They had already been through it with me.

That was not the case for many of my other colleagues in other parts of the school building. So, when I began to get my "sea legs" and venture out into the school again, I often came face-to-face with a colleague or school employee for whom I was the embodiment of their own fears and pain from September 11th. These first meetings were difficult. I absorbed everyone else's emotions, and they were extremely emotional when they saw me.

Some people were struck dumb and didn't know what to say.

Others, predictably, said too much and gave me their unwanted advice.

"You'll be fine."

"Just be strong."

"We've all been through a terrible time."

We? I thought to myself. Well, yes, we had all suffered a terrible tragedy. But it seemed that if there exists something like emotional parity, we were not there. Not yet, anyway.

When I said something to my team teachers about the crazy advice I was receiving, one of them said, "Well, how would you like people to respond to seeing you again?"

I thought about that question for a moment. How should people respond to me? "I guess, what I'd really like is for people to believe in me and my ability to get through all this."

My colleagues smiled. They knew, like I did, that I had all the resources inside me to cope with this time. I just wanted everyone else to know that, too.

And to believe it like I did.

Nothing bothered me as much as someone coming up to me with "that look" on their face and saying, "I don't know how you're doing it. If it were me, I'd pull the covers over my head."

Whatever their intent, the message they were giving me was that what I was going through was somehow perceived to be beyond the human ability to heal—and that was what I knew I needed to do. Heal.

Once the immediate "fog" of September 11th had begun to lift, I had two focuses—finding Ira, and healing myself and my family. The further we came from that terrible day, the more my attention shifted toward healing.

Healing began to mean letting go. Far from "doing" anything, I had to learn to *not* do anything. To let go. However, before I would really be able to do that, I knew I was going to have to find Ira.

My friend Marilyn continues to tell me to this day that I never wavered in my determination to "get through this."

"From the moment the planes hit, you were single-minded in knowing you would get through this tragedy."

She's right. I made a conscious decision to not only "get through" the horrible tragedy but to do so with "flying colors." I knew that anything less than that would discredit Ira and be hurtful to my sons.

I would get through it. *We* would get through it.

So, there were those who couldn't see that I would get through the tragedy—but there were many others who were able to see me, my determination and my strength clearly. One friend, a wonderful physician I know, saw me for the first time about a week after the

Trade Center came down. As soon as she saw me, she hurried toward me and wrapped her arms around me in a warm hug.

"You'll be all right," she told me.

I stepped back and looked at her. "How do you know?"

She smiled at me. "Because you have a buoyant personality."

Now *that* was the kind of thing that I needed to hear. Comments like that were like life preservers tossed to me. By recognizing a strength within me, she bolstered that strength.

This wonderful lady's comment gave me hope. Not the hope for a miracle that my life would somehow be put back together, that Ira would be found and we could pretend that September 11th never happened. That hope was little more than desperation.

I understood that more and more.

No, the "hope" that I was relying on was the hope that I would be able to move forward, that I would be able to recreate my world anew—a world that would be healthy and supportive for my sons and myself, a world that had all the qualities of the world that Ira and I had built together but which I now had to build alone.

Truth be known, it is that kind of hope that has motivated me to write this book.

None of us can return to September 10, 2001. I will never again be able to sit cross-legged on my bed and attempt Deepak Chopra's meditation while Ira gets ready for work. To hope that I could is futile. It is an illusion, one that only limits me.

But to hope to recreate the world so that it embraces all that was good about the world before September 11th and then some… well, *that's* a hope worth having.

CHAPTER FIFTEEN

Memorial and Recovery

When I have a young student who doubts her ability to understand something, the most important thing I can do for her, even more important than explaining again and again, is encourage her. I need to reassure her that she *can* and she *will* understand.

Encouragement is preparing the "soil" of the soul for the seeds that will be planted there.

My advice to anyone visiting someone who has suffered a loss is simple: encourage, encourage, encourage. Identify their positive and powerful qualities, and continually show them how those qualities are anchors, lifelines, tools and gifts.

But don't expect the lesson to be learned quickly or easily. Grief has its own contours and geography. There are moments when it seems that everything will be "all right" and other moments when despair seems the only logical response. Tears are painful, but they are also healing.

In the days and weeks after September 11th, I moved forward shakily. I was like a baby learning to walk. A couple of steps forward represented a major accomplishment. Mostly, I fell. And when I did remain on my feet, I generally had to be holding firm to something or someone.

There was no longer any question about whether Ira perished in the terrorist attack. I had accepted the finality of Ira's death. On some level, I had no choice but to do so. The mundane aspects of the tragedy were brought home to me on an almost daily basis.

When I returned home from teaching, I would invariably find a 9/11–related phone message waiting for me. I had to probate Ira's will. There were other, seemingly trivial matters that had to be taken care of. The checking account had to be switched into my name alone. Mortgage notices. Utility bills.

Time waits for no one.

It is true.

Every day after school, I faced paperwork and phone calls. There were dinners to make, to go to, to miss.

There were always family and friends.

And there was a memorial service to plan.

Did I cry during those many days? Yes. I still do. But I kept busy, and my tears have been intermittent. I managed to take care of all my responsibilities and then collapse into my bed, exhausted. I had no problem sleeping. I was too exhausted to do anything but sleep.

But I didn't feel rested.

I told my sister that I needed to get away, to clear my head a little.

"How about Montauk?" she suggested.

Montauk. The far end of Long Island. How wonderful that sounded! We agreed to go for a weekend in early November. I now had something to look forward to and not just something to "plan for."

Still, I hardly felt "normal." I was easily dehydrated. I'd lost some weight. I didn't feel comfortable "in my body"—using the phrase one massage therapist used to describe what I was feeling.

It took a vigorous one-hour massage to feel my legs again. Can you imagine? Walking around for all those days and feeling a pervading numbness. My stamina was shot.

The thought of exercising tired me out. However, my friends refused to accept my excuses and insisted that I go out for walks with them. Which I did, and which made me feel much better.

I resumed my favorite yoga asanas at home in the mornings. I tried to remain conscious of what I ate and how often.

Despite the "onslaught" of everyday demands, I often found simple tasks difficult to attend to, such as food shopping and cleaning.

After about three weeks, I was food shopping by myself. A small victory, but a real one!

Looking back, I can see that I was still in shock. My body was moving and attending to the things that needed to be attended to, but my soul and mind remained two to three steps behind. Even my grief was playing catch-up.

I knew that part of my difficulty was "closure." When others had suffered a loss of a loved one, they had a funeral, a chance to say goodbye to their loved one. Burying a loved one was important.

Even the rituals associated with burial aid in that sense of closure. In Judaism, mourners are encouraged to assist in putting shovelfuls of dirt into the grave. The thud of the dirt against the casket, though painful to hear, is the beginning of a long goodbye.

I knew with every fiber of my being that until Ira's remains were found, my sons and I would not be able to truly come to terms with our great loss.

One other aspect of my being that was coming to the fore was my sense of Jewishness. I had always felt comfortable with my Jewish identity. Growing up in New York, it was easy to have a comfortable Jewish identity. As Lenny Bruce once said, "If you live in New York, you're Jewish." But this terrible tragedy had given me insight into my Jewish soul and the presence of God in my life.

My husband and the thousands of others who died in the terrorist attack call attention to the fact that there is much too much hatred in the world, too much violence. And while we need to prevent other terrorist attacks, we need to remember that we are all part of the One, all children of God, and each of us deserves to live in peace.

My only problem was how to say goodbye.

The day of the memorial service was approaching. Even as we prepared the service, I was meeting with the grief counselor provided by Lehman Brothers. His goal for me was to resume my life. He strongly encouraged my return to work.

It seemed that, to him, returning to work was an indication that I was functioning "well."

That makes me laugh now, to think that I was functioning well during those days and weeks. Still, he and I were in total agreement about getting back to my life. I very much wanted to be thought of as "doing well," and I took on the responsibility for doing that.

Rabbi Lavin offered the synagogue for the memorial service, which was good because it could hold over a thousand people. Ira's former boss, Karen Krieger, arranged for our family in Florida to be hooked up to the service via teleconferencing equipment.

I wanted to look my best for the service. My dear friend Arlene and I went shopping, searching the entire north shore of Long Island until we found the perfect suit.

Finding a place to hold the service and finding an outfit to wear were easy. The real difficulty was emotional.

Before the service, I spoke to both my sons. "Have you decided what you'd like to say?" I asked them.

They both had given a great deal of thought to their respective speeches. They knew that this would be their one chance to publicly proclaim what their father had meant to them. They wanted to memorialize their father and the beautiful life he lived. I must say that my fine young men both rose to the occasion with heartfelt and unique perspectives on their relationships with their father.

My thoughts were too jumbled to put on paper. In fact, I didn't write my speech until the night before the service. I was concerned about being calm and poised. I certainly didn't want to "lose it" in front of everyone. But I didn't know how I'd avoid being too emotional.

While I was struggling with this issue, the phone rang. It was Neil Goodman, Ira's friend since childhood. He couldn't have called at a more opportune time. He and I spoke about the spiritual aspects of 9/11, that there was a reason for the event, beyond "our reason." We spoke about where Ira is now, and I found myself being comforted by Neil's strong beliefs in the hereafter. Neil had enough experiences with the world of spirit to convince him that it existed and that life continued beyond the physical body.

I have always shared Neil's feelings, but I was in so much pain, I couldn't eliminate the painful feelings on my own. Speaking with Neil did that for me.

The morning of the service dawned bright and clear. When it was my time to speak, I looked out at the sea of faces and felt a calm come over me. I spoke from my heart with my sons standing on either side of me. At one point, when I did choke up, I felt both of their hands lovingly on my back.

My sons spoke, followed by my sister and my Uncle Murray. He was followed by some of Ira's friends and colleagues.

And then it was time for *shiva*, the seven-day mourning period. I had bristled not that long before when someone brought cake to my house. Then, I still held out hope that Ira would be found alive. But now, I was reconciled that he would not be.

Although *shiva* is only seven days, it seemed to have lasted from September to the end of November. After the memorial service, things seemed to calm down, but then I learned that Mayor Giuliani was planning a special ceremony on October 28th for the families of those who had not yet found their loved ones. At that time, each family would receive an urn with soil from Ground Zero.

I was initially upset by this thought. I wanted my husband's body, and all I would have was an urn of dirt? But, if that was all I *could* have, then it was what I would take.

However, with each passing day, I grew more and more upset. My Jewish identity seemed to cry to me to have a body to bury. How could I find comfort with dirt in an urn?

I prayed and prayed, seeking an answer to my dilemma and some comfort for my soul.

A friend of mine suggested I visit the grave of Rabbi Schneerson, the Grand Hasidic Rebbe. Many of his followers thought he was the messiah. Even after his death, there are many who believe that he had a "direct line to God" and that praying at his grave would help.

I decided that I would travel to Queens and to the Rebbe's grave as soon as I was able.

Meanwhile, the next day, October 25th, I agreed to go to the boardwalk during lunchtime to walk with my friends and team teachers. However, I felt tired almost as soon as we began, and I sat down on a bench.

"You go ahead without me," I told them. "I'll catch up or be here when you come back."

As they started to head further down the boardwalk, I suddenly got the feeling that I had to call home. I ignored the feeling for a while, and then I called to my friends that I was just going down to my car for a minute. There, I dialed my house on my cell phone.

My son Adam picked up the phone. "Mom, did you get my message?"

"What message?"

"Two detectives are here from the Fourth Precinct."

"What happened?"

"They found Dad. Your principal is out looking for you now."

I jumped into my car and began to honk my horn, getting my friends' attention. I was crying tears of joy when they made their way to the car.

"What's happened?" they asked.

"God is good," was all I could say in reply. "God is good."

CHAPTER SIXTEEN

Cemetery Shopping

Finding Ira's body meant that I could finally have "closure" to this difficult time in my life and the lives of my family members. Once we'd had a funeral, then the grieving and healing process could begin.

However, before we finally reached that point, there were a couple of emotional hurdles still to be gotten over.

My rabbi advised me to make funeral arrangements, so I asked my friend Marilyn if she would go with me to the funeral chapel, the same one where I'd had my mother's funeral. As difficult as that was, returning to the chapel and those sad memories, the people working there were very professional and considerate. They knew exactly what had to be done to ensure that Ira's body would be sent there.

As the funeral director looked over the paperwork, he noted that we had never purchased a plot.

"We'd never thought..." I said, looking away.

"No problem, really," he said, his voice smooth and calming. "I would suggest, since you have to go to the cemetery to select a plot anyway, that you go look at Mount Ararat. That's just down the road from where your family is buried, and that way, if you are visiting, it will be easy to visit everyone."

Although there was a certain logic to that suggestion, I didn't see why we shouldn't just look at Beth Moses Cemetery, which is where my family is actually buried.

Marilyn offered to have Howie accompany me on the trip to the cemetery, but I declined.

"I think that Adam and I should go," I said.

"You're sure?"

I nodded. "Yes, I think so."

When Adam and I arrived at Beth Moses, we were taken to a quiet room where the salesperson—I suppose he was a salesperson, although that seems a strange way to describe what he was selling—took out what looked like a family photo album and showed us a photograph of two adjacent plots.

"These have just been sold back to us. The owners had purchased them years ago, but now they live in Florida and would like to have plots there."

Because the plots had been purchased so long before, they were located quite close to the cemetery office. A good location?

"Easy to find and get to," Adam said.

However, I wasn't thinking about the location. In order to purchase the plot for Ira, I would have to purchase the other one as well. Both or nothing. However, the thought of purchasing my own plot was too disturbing for me to consider rationally.

"Buy a grave for myself? I'm only fifty-two!"

"Mom," Adam said, trying to calm me down, "the whole family is here. I feel comfortable visiting here. Why would you want to look anywhere else?"

"No. We'll see what there is at Mount Ararat." I was motivated by my emotions as well as by my experience as a shopper. Real estate might be defined by "location, location, location," but good deals are found by "shop around, shop around."

Mount Ararat was as impressive to behold as the funeral director suggested. More than a "cemetery," it billed itself as a "memorial park." It was as pleasant as it could be. And I liked the way it was laid out.

A well-coiffed woman met us in the well-decorated office. Having a woman there seemed to put me at ease. When I explained that I was looking for a single plot, she had a man come in and then guide us to the area where she thought we would be most comfortable.

We drove along the roads, following his directions, and then we got out and looked around. It was truly beautiful. The only problem was, we didn't know anyone there, and we ended up leaving with a cold feeling.

When I got back to the car, I called my Aunt Essie on my cell. "What should I do?" I asked her, my emotions making my voice tight as I explained my dilemma. "How can I buy two graves? That's like saying that my own death is going to be soon. I don't want to die."

"Oh please, Felice," she said, her voice a perfect balance of reassurance and dismissiveness of my *mishagas* (craziness). "First of all, you're not going to die anytime soon, so calm down. Buying two graves doesn't mean you're going to die. Rose has been married to her second husband, Hank, for twenty-five years, and she bought two graves when Larry died.

"You're just shaken up. Take a deep breath and relax."

I did exactly as she said. As I did, I realized that I was upset because this whole process was forcing me to confront something more than Ira's funeral. At the same time, it was forcing me to confront my own mortality.

"Go back to Beth Moses," my Uncle Murray yelled in the background. "The whole *mishpucha* (family) is there."

So, back to Beth Moses it was. Ira is buried there, in a fine location right next to the plot reserved for me.

And after the funeral, once I knew that Ira could rest in peace, I could turn my attention to healing.

BOOK TWO

... To Healing

CHAPTER SEVENTEEN

Bloom Where You Are Planted

From here to ... to what? September 11th was such a profoundly hurtful event in the lives of all of us who experienced it that it's hard to imagine how we've managed to move forward day by day, let alone how we could ever face a future. So many of us feel weighted down by the incredible weight of that hurt.

For all of us, the hurt was deep.

For me and so many others, the hurt was also personal and intimate.

Either way, we all need to find a way to go from the hurt to ... healing. We owe it to ourselves and to all the wonderful people whose lives were stolen by the events of that day. To *not* heal would lock us into pain and hurt. And then the terrorists win.

We owe it to ourselves and to our loved ones to heal.

But how?

For me, the answer began with a quote that was shared with me a number of years earlier by a friend and colleague of the Long Island Writing Project. Anne Marie and I were sitting near one another after a break in the session focused on "sayings and phrases that are meaningful to you" when she turned to me and said, "Bloom where you are planted."

I turned to her. "I beg your pardon?"

She smiled. "That's the quote I'm thinking of."

"What was it again?"

"Bloom where you are planted."

Many times in the hours, days and weeks since September 11th, I have found that phrase entering my consciousness. *Bloom where you are planted.* It has such an earthy, healthy quality to it. From the first time I heard it, I liked the way it sounded. The phrasing of it, the immediate image that came into my mind of my small garden. Flowers. Lush lawns. Nesting.

But, in the desperate and lost days and weeks after September 11th, the phrase took on a new meaning. *Bloom where you are planted.* No one can be what they're not. "There's nothing you can do that can't be done," John Lennon sang in "All You Need Is Love."

So many people want to be something they're not—which is much different from being "more" than you ever thought you were. But the path to achieving greater things must always go through where you are. No one can build dreams upon what "should" be. You can only build upon what "is."

Going forward for me had to begin with where I was, not where I *wanted* to be. Where I wanted to be was simple. I wanted to be in the world that existed before September 11th. The only trouble was, that world no longer existed. Everything I'd dreamt of with Ira, everything that we'd planned, everything that we'd built together was gone.

I could still have dreams and plans. I still had a future. But the world that had been "we," me and Ira, was gone.

And that had to be my starting point. If it wasn't, then I knew I would be doomed to an endless loop of sadness and pain.

Most people do not move forward, because they never seem to get comfortable in where they are. And I understand that. I understand it more deeply than I'd ever wanted to understand it. But I was now in a post–September 11th world. I was in a world that no longer had Ira coming home from work every day. I was no longer in a world of "we."

I was now in a world of "me."

And nothing affirmed that reality more than finally having a funeral for Ira.

As we followed the rabbi's invitation to place a shovelful of dirt upon the lowered casket, a ritual that brings home very concretely the finality of a funeral, Anne Marie's words came back to me and filled my mind. "Bloom where you are planted."

I smiled to myself. I smiled to myself through my tears.

"What's the matter, Mom?" Adam asked, leaning close to me.

I turned to look at him. I saw the worried look in his eyes. I wanted to reassure him. I patted his hand. "Nothing's the matter," I told him honestly.

And nothing *was* the matter. With Anne Marie's words in my mind, I glanced down at Ira's casket, partially covered by dirt, and I realized that I would bloom and that this spot was where I was planted.

I could *want* things to be different, but the simple fact was that *this* was my new starting point. This is where I was planting.

And from this reality was where I would bloom.

I realized that I had understood that wisdom of Anne Marie's words fully when I happened to bump into her several weeks later. It was just after I'd come out of my yoga class, when I stopped into a nearby store for a salad. I was coming around the far end of the salad bar when I suddenly found myself face-to-face with Anne Marie.

Unlike some people, who had avoided running into me because of their own discomfort, Anne Marie smiled genuinely when she saw me. A pretty woman with soft features framed by short, dark hair, she carried herself smoothly and walked toward me with purpose. She came closer and embraced me warmly.

"This is *bashert!*" I exclaimed.

It had been over two years since we'd seen one another. Yet she had been one of the people most in my thoughts during the past few weeks.

"I wanted to call you," she began. "But I didn't know what to say."

All I could do was smile. "You'd already said more than you can ever understand," I told her.

"I've prayed for you often," she told me. "And on a gut level, I knew that everything would be all right with you."

"You did?" I asked curiously. "How was that?"

"Because you are such a spiritual person. You can find truth and meaning even in this terrible tragedy."

I told her it was amazing that we had bumped into one another just then, because I had been thinking about her so much—and about the wisdom of the words she'd spoken to me so long before I could appreciate how significant they would become to me.

Her eyes brightened. "You are amazing," she said.

I looked, genuinely confused by her words.

"Who else could have taken those words and made them real in such a positive way—at such a difficult time of their life?"

I shrugged. The words had "spoken" themselves to me. I didn't think I had done anything. But maybe that was the spirituality that she'd spoken about.

I have learned that things are said at a particular time for a particular purpose, and we simply have to open ourselves to "hearing" the words so that their meaning can be clear to us.

So many things have been said to me during the past year, things that could not have been said—or, more correctly, I could not have fully understood—at any other time.

Another example was in my reconnecting with an old friend who I had originally met the summer of 1965—the very same summer when I met Ira! I found Chuck to be a wonderful and supportive friend, someone whose voice was so healing for me to hear at this time in my life. Clear and confident when he spoke, he delivered some important messages.

During one particular conversation, he and I were talking about how horrible my loss was when he suddenly stopped and looked me straight in the eyes. "You know what I think?" he said.

I shook my head.

"I think that life is good and that you deserve to be happy."

His simple observation stunned me with its obvious truth. My God! What an impact those few words had on me just then. So many of my friends who cared so deeply about me cried with me, hugged me, bemoaned my fate with me.

But Chuck was having none of that. Equally caring and supportive, he refused to sink down with me. Rather, he insisted on rising up with me. He looked at the bright side of life, something I was desperate to do at that point. I knew I had to get above my grief and sadness. I could already feel it pulling me down into a sadness that was larger than anything I had ever known.

"Fine and good," I told him on another occasion. "But this wasn't a personal tragedy alone. Those murdering terrorists committed a terrible crime against all good and innocent people..."

He raised his hand gently to silence me. "I don't disagree with your feelings," he said. "But tell me, what good does it do for you to feel such anger? There's nothing you can do about it."

Not feel anger? What other response was there? But then I recalled the Serenity Prayer written by Reinhold Niebuhr: "God, grant me the serenity to accept the things I cannot change, courage to change the things I can, and wisdom to know the difference."

Chuck was providing me with the "wisdom" to tell the difference in this particular situation. What he meant by his observation, "There's nothing you can do about it," cut right to the core of what I was expressing.

In fact, I was not railing against the terrorists and their murderous act. I was railing against the world that had changed under my feet. I was railing against the loss of my Ira.

And Chuck was saying that while I could take some political action to oppose terrorism, there was nothing I could do to bring my husband back.

And that was the real source of my anger.

Another friend I happened to run into one day observed that Ira and I were so close.

"You were joined spiritually as husband and wife. The way he was torn from you has created a spiritual wound that has torn you apart.

"Your job is to become whole again."

How I needed to hear that very sentiment! It validated my own feelings that were forming in my mind. Losing a beloved spouse in such a violent, wrenching manner is like having a part of your body suddenly ripped from you. I had truly lost my "other half."

My job was to heal myself.

Bloom where you are planted.

After Ira's body was recovered and I'd selected a plot, we had a small, intimate funeral. About forty members of our family, some close friends. No one else. The rabbi conducted a brief, dignified service.

He noted that it was important for Jews to bury their dead.

He spoke of the Bar Kochba Revolt that occurred nearly two thousand years ago. Burdened by the cruelty of the Hadrianic persecutions, the Jewish general Simon Bar Kochba (Son of a Star) led the Jews in revolt against the authorities. Many Jews were slaughtered, both in the fighting and in punishment for the revolt.

However, despite their cruelty, the Romans allowed the Jewish people to bury their dead. And because of this, the rabbis added a new blessing that is recited after meals: "God is good. He does good."

The rabbis of that time, like the rabbis of today, sought to find some good even in the most horrific of tragedies. There was little to find in the consequences of the Bar Kochba Revolt, yet they found this.

Because they knew that, absent a body for burial as proof that a death actually took place, the women who had been married to the brave Jews who had sought to throw off the yoke of Roman persecution would have been considered "agunas" prohibited from remarrying.

Without a burial, without proof of a husband's death, the women were still considered to be married, and therefore unable to marry again. Sadly, this was the fate of so many young women who had managed to survive the Holocaust. Their husbands had died in the camps or in the streets, but there was no official record and no burial. As a result, Jewish law did not permit them to remarry.

Thus, while they had managed to somehow escape the terrible fire of the Holocaust, they were forever after limited in their ability to seek and find solace in rebuilding their lives.

I had been spared a similar fate.

"God is good."

The remainder of the funeral service was beautiful. Ira was buried with prayer books, an honor in the Jewish religion, and I was handed the American flag that had been draped over him when he had been removed from the rubble of the Twin Towers.

Planted, I was ready to bloom.

CHAPTER EIGHTEEN

Grieving

After the funeral, the grieving process really began.

Too many people are uncomfortable with grief because they do not understand what it is. Grieving, while painful, is different from sadness. Grieving is the beginning of emotional healing; sadness is simply a painful place to be.

"Grieving well" is an intensely personal and fulfilling process. Just as the burn victim screams in physical agony as his body heals, the grieving person cries in psychic agony as her soul begins to mend.

I knew I would never hold my husband in my arms again. Never again speak with him. Never again hear his voice. All the things we had dreamed of doing together would never be done. All the things we had planned together would not be realized.

This was what was. The real deal. Truth. Ugly, painful, heart-wrenching reality.

This was my life.

My world was not always a nice place to visit.

My sister and I took that trip to Montauk, on the easternmost point of Long Island, during the first weekend in November, following the funeral. We walked around Gurney's Inn and sat looking out at the sea as the brisk sunshine glimmered off the waves.

It was beautiful.

Heartrendingly beautiful.

I cried.

I was not there with Ira. I would never again sit on a beach and reach my hand out to his. Every beautiful view, every moment of joy was tinged with sadness for me. I cried when I should have smiled, laughed when I should have been silent.

Michele did not know how to handle these raw emotions. She was frightened by my feelings laid so bare. I was aware of her discomfort, but I was powerless to handle myself any differently. There was no guile. No forethought. Just emotional reaction.

I had no choice but to "let it all hang out." Perhaps it upset her even more since I am her older sister and had always been the "strong one."

Michele was at a loss as to what to say to me or how to react.

"Have you spoken to a therapist?" was one question that she asked a lot. That and, "Do you think you should try some medication?"

No! My problem was not medication, it was reality. How I wanted to scream at her—but I love her dearly and knew that she simply had no way of understanding what I was going through. She did not have the tools to deal with my grief any more effectively than she was doing.

"You cannot medicate grief," I observed.

"But medication could take the edge off. It could help you feel better in order to deal with your feelings..."

I shook my head. "For me, it would only make my grief less authentic. And I could never bear that."

We live in a culture that is too quick to medicate, to "take the edge off," to deny feelings. But grief is the process of facing inconceivable feelings face-to-face. It is in the raw pain that healing begins.

Medicating, hiding, denying... these things simply make it harder to heal in the long run. And life is always lived in a balance of the here and now and the long term.

For me, grief would build up in my throat and chest until I couldn't stand it anymore. Then I would cry. Sometimes my crying would be brief, like a passing summer squall. Other times my crying would seem to linger on and on, like a deep storm system.

As upsetting as these periods were to Michele, they helped me feel "normal." They were not pleasant, but they felt right. They felt honest. They felt true.

And I needed to get to that honesty, because I knew that healing was there. That weekend was very healing for me. Not only did I have a massage, which helped remove some of the tension from my body, but Michele and I had many conversations, the like of which we'd never had before.

We talked about my boys and how best to help them get through this terrible time. We imagined together how I would rebuild my life as a single woman.

We also talked about what Ira's death meant to her. After all, I was not the only one who was grieving on that trip. She had lost a brother-in-law who had been like a brother to her.

By the end of the weekend, I was feeling more grounded. Poor Michele was probably a good deal more stressed from having to deal with me in a grief state. But after all, what are sisters for if not that kind of support?

Spending time with Michele was one of the positive consequences of what had happened. I spent a lot of time with her during those first few months. She came from Manhattan regularly and stayed over a lot. We went to movies. We had dinner out. We talked and shopped.

And shopped.

And shopped.

During one of these shopping expeditions, we found ourselves in a lingerie store. I grew teary-eyed as I looked at all the beautiful sleepwear. I was looking at all the delicate and sensual lingerie and feeling such a profound and physical loss.

Michele seemed to sense what I needed. She nudged me and told me she knew just what I needed. She led me in the direction of the pajamas. There, she found the cuddliest pair of pajamas which she bought for me.

"One step at a time," she said knowingly.

I wanted to be with my sister as much as possible. She sensed when I was in the most pain, and she did more than tolerate it, she found some way of letting me express it safely. She stayed close. She made herself available for me all the time.

Our parents are both deceased, and we are the only ones left of our birth family. Having that connection was so important for me.

It was very important for Adam, as well. Still at home, he was comforted by Michele being with us. She became a rock for both of us.

As New Year's Eve approached, I wanted desperately to be with my sister.

I was not in a partying mood yet, so I certainly did not plan on going out to paint the town. She knew that and returned home early from a ski trip in order to be with me. Our roles had shifted so seamlessly. For that short time, she had become my big sister, taking care of me.

And I had become like the little sister, needing to be taken care of.

CHAPTER NINETEEN

Healing Begins

As much as I benefited from being with Michele, there was a limit to what she could do. There wasn't a lot people could do "for me." Keep me busy. Keep me distracted. Listen when I needed to talk. Talk when I needed to listen. But, ultimately, the healing I needed had to come from within me, not from anyone else.

Any help I needed with that process had to come from people who were either walking that path with me or who had already gone down that road.

It was during this time that I decided on my personal least favorite word in the English language—*widow*. How I came to hate that word. Not only did it have a miserable sound, everything that it connoted and denoted was miserable. And I did not want to be miserable.

Of course, I also did not want to be a widow.

But that was precisely what I was.

A number of women who had lost their husbands approached me during those months to give me advice, insight, comfort or words of strength.

My late mother had many friends, and some of these wonderful friends were women she had grown up with. One of them was Rose. Rose had lost her first husband, Larry, at a very young age, much too young an age to be a widow. Both of them were in their thirties.

When she became a widow, she had two school-aged children and little money. She had little of what most people think is necessary to get along in the world. However, she had one thing in abundance that too many people are lacking—a powerful life force, a *joie de vivre*.

When I think of Rose, I always picture her at weddings and Bar Mitzvahs as the first one on the dance floor and the last to leave. She was determined to get as much joy from life as possible. She was candid in her views and comfortable speaking her mind, no matter whose feelings got in the way.

"I speak my mind and let the chips fall where they may," she said more than once.

Ira and I both enjoyed her company and her sincerity. In fact, unlike the people who were uncomfortable with her openness, we adored her.

Not long after September 11th, Rose called me. She apologized for not calling sooner, but she said that she'd wanted to give me some time. "I knew you would be swamped with people and things to do."

Of course, she was one hundred percent right. We talked for a long time, and I was comforted listening to her. She spoke with the voice of life experience, directly and confidently.

"Listen to me, Felice," she said. "Right now, you need a mother's voice, but your mother isn't here, so you'll have to make do with me."

Her words hit me. She was right. I did need a mother's voice. And I was more than willing to make do with hers.

"Listen to what I'm saying. If it sounds harsh, don't worry. Just know that I know what I'm talking about. Okay?"

"Okay, Rose."

"Right now, your first concern has to be yourself and your children. Nothing else matters. Nothing. Do you hear? No one else's feelings. Nothing."

I nodded. "Yes, of course."

"Okay. Now, I want you to get all of Ira's clothes out of your house."

"What? Why?"

"You'll feel better."

"How? I don't understand."

"Felice, as long as his clothes are there, you can smell him. He's too much *there*. As long as his clothes are there, it's like he's still alive. And, Felice, he's not still alive."

Although there was a part of me that wanted to resist, I knew she was right. The bedroom I'd shared all these years with Ira was now mine alone. The same was true of the entire house.

It was up to me to claim it now.

I had to claim my life as a single person. No one else was going to claim it for me, that was for sure.

Rose checked in on me with some regularity, reminding me to get rid of his things. I knew she was right, but it was hard. I wanted to be ready.

"You'll never be ready. Just do it."

With the help of my friends Naomi and Marilyn, I followed Rose's advice.

I got rid of his shoes first because, traditionally, shoes are not given to anyone close to the deceased person.

I threw away things that couldn't be donated—underwear and socks. Then I invited the boys to come and take whatever they wanted of their father's. "Keep what feels good to you," I told them.

Bryan kept Ira's ski jacket; Adam took a new suit that he altered to fit him. I kept Ira's favorite sweatpants and a couple of sweatshirts, one that said "Maine," purchased on a vacation. I found it hard to part with his raincoat, which I wore to temple one rainy day. "That was Ira's, wasn't it?" my friend Steve asked, recognizing the tan coat and its oversize on me.

After the boys had taken what they wanted, I packed up everything else. Taped the boxes shut. And then stacked them.

The clothes were out of the drawers and the closets, but I couldn't quite get them out of the house—not yet. I worried that the boys might change their minds and want something that they'd left behind.

Finally, I donated everything.

The house seemed larger. Now it was only me and my things filling it.

I painted the bedroom, bought new carpeting and bedding, and did whatever I could to make it feel completely mine.

Rose had been right. I did feel better.

What felt the best was knowing that there was an older, wiser woman who cared about me enough to tell me like it was, who would give me good, solid advice no matter how painful to follow.

Rose continues to give me great advice and insight. She is a sounding board for me when it comes to dating and dealing with men. We talk about the past and the people we loved. The best part was that Rose always made me laugh, even at the lowest points.

She was an example and role model for me. She'd been dealt an equally difficult hand. Maybe her loss was not as public, or wrapped in national tragedy, but it was just as painful for her.

All real loss is personal, after all.

Rose faced her loss and then carried on. She married a wonderful man and continues on, with her energy and joy, helping me and others.

Sue was another source of good advice. I have known Sue for many years. She worked in the school where I taught. She had lost her husband a number of years earlier. When she learned that I'd lost Ira in the terrorist attack, she wrote me a lovely note and invited me to talk whenever I needed to.

I took her up on that invitation, because she was a woman I liked and admired. In addition to being a fine elementary school teacher, she was the mother of two grown children and the grandmother of five. She seemed always to be in control of her life.

When her husband passed away suddenly, I observed her closely and felt that she had maintained her dignity and independence, moving forward to continue a good life for herself. She connected with a bereavement group and established friendships, retired from teaching when she felt ready and moved to an adult community not far from her children. She enjoyed her life there, taking pleasure in being with family and enjoying the activities in her community.

Because her husband had died so suddenly, she was able to relate in some way to my own loss.

"The first thing you should do is make some single friends. Your married friends will be great, but you will want people who are more flexible to do things and travel with."

How right she was!

She also recommended that I participate in a bereavement group.

"But I am doing well, mourning Ira."

"Bereavement groups aren't just for mourning," she pointed out. "They are wonderful ways to make some important social connections with people who are going through the same things you're going through."

Once again, she was right on target. There are a number of people from my bereavement group who I remain in close touch with. I learned from these women that we shared the same concerns. With guidance from our leader, we discussed our next steps as they appeared.

Sue was more than a great source of spoken advice. She was a great role model as well. She kept her house, made new friends, took care of her children and grandchildren, maintained her career and, when she was ready for a relationship, connected with a wonderful gentleman.

Louise, the girlfriend of my father-in-law, was another wonderful source of support and caring. Louise had also experienced the loss of a beloved spouse. She had a sixth sense of knowing when I would be feeling down, and she made a point of calling at just the right time.

All these women taught me the absolute truth of the old saying: "Those who say it cannot be done should not interrupt the person doing it."

I knew that everyone meant well when they gave advice, but much of the advice was born from timidity. I did not want to hear about how to become less than everything I could be. When someone said to me, "Well, I guess you will have to find some other women in your situation to do things with," or "Sometimes a woman gets lucky and finds a man who also has had a loss..." Oy vey!

If I didn't pull my covers over my head after September 11th, I wasn't about to do so now. I had planted, now I was looking to bloom!

I had no time or patience for pessimism. My glass was half full.

Of all the advice—good and bad—that I had been given, the advice I relied on most of all was the advice I didn't receive, advice I only imagined:

What would Ira say?

I believed he would urge me to go out and have a good time. He knew I would anyway. He'd always thought of me as optimistic.

"You're irrepressible," he would tell me. He always thought I was tenacious. He would tell me to hang in there. To stick it out. To be happy.

I would handle my loss my way. And I was going to be what I was going to be—a strong, healthy, independent woman.

I am not pretending that I wasn't scared, that the future didn't look ominous. I worried about who would love me and who would care about me. I wasn't eighteen anymore.

I knew that where I'd once had plans, I was now confronting a blank page.

I knew how much more my boys would depend on me now.

And me... what about my future?

One of Ira's friends at Lehman told me how often Ira talked about how it was going to be when we retired. He was really looking forward to that time. And so was I. We spoke about traveling when I retired and the places we wished to go. We thought we would keep our home and travel to warm places in the winter.

But now what?

Now I would have to confront a new plan, one of my own devising.

The first thing I had to do was believe I could have a plan. Believe in myself. And once I did that, slowly but surely, I began to emerge. Not the Felice I had been for so many years. That Felice was part of a couple. This "new" Felice was a single, independent and strong woman.

Slowly, I was regaining my energy. My desire to build my life was coming back.

I was becoming more and more aware of how many people cared about me and my family, how many people were putting in the time and energy to help.

And I was also becoming more and more aware of just how much Ira had loved me. So many people shared touching stories of Ira and me, and the love that was evident between us. A colleague recalled running into us at Roosevelt Field Mall. She described how we sat on a bench, taking a break from shopping, my legs resting on his knees. "You looked so close and loving," she said.

Ira had once told the boys that the key to success was knowing what you want. He then told them that I was a person who knew what I wanted and, because of that, I was always successful. He also told the boys that I was his best asset.

I wanted to honor Ira's memory and ideals by continuing to be the person he'd known me to be. Beneath the grief, the pain, the anguish, I had a powerful desire to stand up tall, to live life and to be happy again.

I felt the love and pride—and relief—of my sons when I took control of my life and helped them with theirs.

I couldn't let them down.

I couldn't let *me* down.

And I wouldn't. For the first time in my child-rearing years, I was going to put myself first. Our sons were adults. Whatever Ira could have given them, he had given them. They would never be "fatherless," because he'd been such a powerful presence in their lives. Of course, they would have been better off with him there, but they were going to be fine.

In fact, Bryan had already begun to articulate his grief in positive ways, ways that Ira would understand and be proud of. He founded a charity called the Ira Zaslow Foundation. He organized a number of fundraisers and contributed the money raised to good causes. One of the fundraisers was Team Ira. Together with other runners, Bryan finished seven marathons. A playground was built in memory of Ira at Temple Hillel in North Woodmere. The Foundation donated computers and other needed tools to an inner-city school.

Bryan and Adam at the Elmhurst (Queens) subway stop near Ira's childhood home. Bryan was selected to carry the torch before the 2004 Summer Olympics.

Adam did not show his grief the same way. He spoke of communicating with Ira in his dreams. I remember envying him for his dreams. How I wished to see Ira in mine, but at the time I could not dream. Looking back, I realize that Adam was processing his feelings internally, in his unique way.

Adam went on to create the Aron, Spitz, Zaslow (ASZ) Foundation with his friend Andrew, who had lost his stepfather and brother-in-law on 9/11. They held basketball events, bringing in local college coaches, an array of NBA halftime acts and former NBA players to

Adam (third from right) and Andrew (center) with their family members at an ASZ Foundation event

entertain and hold basketball clinics for youngsters from an organization called Tuesday's Children (tuesdayschildren.org) who had lost loved ones on 9/11. The proceeds were donated to established charitable organizations such as Tuesday's Children and the Boys & Girls Clubs of New York.

Both Bryan and Adam learned to channel their grief in positive ways that helped others. I took great pride in their accomplishments.

Everyone works through grief at individual paces. That is the nature of grief. It is intense. It is intimate. It is powerful.

But, done well, it is healing also.

As I continued to heal, I encouraged myself to enjoy my time alone. Rather than feel sorry for myself for being without my husband, I tried to think of myself as a young woman again, with my life still to unfold before me, filled with possibility.

And that was not untrue! My life was still before me, waiting to unfold in all its brilliant, beautiful and incredible possibilities.

I did things that brought me joy, for no other reason than that they brought me joy. I traveled a fair amount, going to New Mexico because of its beautiful vistas and deep spirituality. I took care of my body, exercising more.

I socialized more, extending myself to interact with new people, and more interesting people. I met friends through ballroom dance classes and dances. I opened up to dating. I even became a bit "rebellious," going to restaurants that I knew Ira wouldn't have liked. There was a restaurant called Apple in Rockville Centre, a town nearby. Ira never wanted to try it. I went there with friends every chance I got and enjoyed the food. Ira would have laughed.

As the months passed, I expressed more and more of myself. I was healing. I could feel it. The sun was beginning to feel warm on my face again. And it made me happy.

Friends who have known me for a long time were amazed at my transformation. "Felice, you've always been active, but now ... !"

I explained to them that, in the past, most of my activity had been directed toward *doing* things; now most of my activity was devoted to *being* me—the me that I now had no choice but to be. I always loved dancing, but now I was doing it regularly, taking classes in ballroom, Latin and even Israeli dancing. I began practicing yoga after many years and joined a gym to work out.

I was determined that my activities would not simply be "diversions" from my grief and sadness. Certainly they were that, but I wanted them to be more. I could have traveled anywhere I wanted, but I traveled to New Mexico, because it is a place of profound spirituality.

My friend Lynda arranged for me to get together with Gail, another woman who was recently widowed. We became friends, and as it happened, Ira and her husband, Stan, had been "train friends." We had already learned a lot about one another and our families because of that connection.

Gail and I went on a group tour of New Mexico, enjoying the huge mountains and ancient Native American culture. There were artifacts and villages to see and gorgeous artwork, like that of Georgia O'Keeffe and R.C. Gorman. I remember taking a gondola ride which went vertically up a mountain and having no fear, relishing the excitement of doing something new and out of my comfort zone. That would have been terrifying in my "old life."

I was finally "stepping out beyond the grief," as psychologists might have expressed it.

How had I managed to reach this level of redemption and hope?

For starters, I was honest with myself and my grief. I never pretended, or tried to pretend, that everything would be "all right." After September 11th, "all right" would have meant back to how things were on September 10th. And that could never be. Not in this world.

So "all right" was not my goal. Honesty was my goal. Genuine grief. Wrestling with my hurt.

You know, it's interesting how important it is to "wrestle" with the things that trouble us rather than avoid them or numb ourselves to them.

Rabbis often speak about the Bible story when Jacob's name was changed from Jacob to Israel. Throughout his life, Jacob's name had been an identifier of how he had actually fallen short of his goals. According to the Biblical account, Jacob and his twin brother, Esau, fought one another in Rebecca's womb—struggling to determine who would be born first and, therefore, be able to claim the birthright and the inheritance right from their father.

The Bible speaks of Rebecca's pain during pregnancy and explains the pain as being the result of this tremendous struggle. Finally, when the twins were born, Esau appeared first—with Jacob so close behind that he was actually grasping Esau's heel. And that is how Jacob earned his name. "Jacob" is derived from the Hebrew word for "heel."

Jacob's life was spent trying to regain the advantage lost to him by that first struggle. He had a powerful supporter in his mother, Rebecca, who preferred Jacob's quiet, gentle ways to his brother's wild, violent ways. However, Isaac, the boys' father, seemed to prefer Esau.

Two events resulted in Jacob "stealing" the birthright from his brother. However, once stolen, he had to go into hiding to avoid his brother's wrath.

As he grew older, with riches, camels and power of his own, he decided it was time to make peace with his brother, so he traveled to his brother's lands to do so. The night before he was to meet up with his brother, the Bible tells us that Jacob was approached by an angel of God. The two of them wrestled throughout the night. The struggle concluded with Jacob being wounded on his thigh, but the fight itself was a draw.

With the dawn of that new day, God blessed Jacob with a new name. No longer signifying his "second place start" in life, his name was changed to "Israel" which means, quite literally, "one who wrestles with God."

Jacob finally found himself, his true self, when he went out to seek peace with his brother. And, in doing so, he "wrestled" with the very nature which had held him back. It was only in the morning, changed as he had to have been by the wound inflicted on him, that he was reborn with his new, truer character and his more accurate name.

My first step toward getting beyond my grief was to allow myself to "wrestle honestly." No holds barred. To me, this meant feeling my feelings when they came up. I learned that grief cannot be avoided. If the pain of it was welling up, I had to allow myself to cry. Feelings pass when acknowledged, and although these were the strongest feelings I have ever felt, I needed to face them. As time went by, they did weaken, as long as they were acknowledged.

Of course, I don't know that I would have been able to do that without the help of some pretty remarkable people. Two of those people are psychologists. Judy and Larry founded a WTC support group which met close to my home on Long Island.

When our meetings began, we were a fairly large group. We gathered at Judy and Larry's home. Spouses. Children. Siblings. We were the hurt and grieving ones who had been left to deal with the horrors of the terrorist attack.

There was one member of our group who was unique, even in our group of unique individuals. We were all "survivors," but unlike the rest of us, being a survivor was different for Mike. We were the surviving family members of those who perished in the terrorist attack. Mike was a real survivor. He had been in the World Trade Center that day. And he had gotten out.

There are those who might think that Mike didn't really belong in a group like ours, that he would become an object of jealousy or envy. *"Why did he survive and my loved one didn't?"* However, Mike was welcomed by all of us. I found him to be a remarkable presence. Not only had he somehow escaped death in the World Trade Center, but he had been present at other disasters and had survived them as well.

To my way of thinking, Mike was with us for a reason—just as he had been at the World Trade Center and the sites of the other disasters for a reason.

He had something to tell us. I looked at this fine young man and saw how much he suffered. He could not look at anything without seeing it through the vision of the Towers coming down around him. He could not listen to a person's voice without hearing the cries for help and the screams of agony that surrounded him that day.

He was meant to live and to bring us a message, if only we had ears to hear.

Some in the group did not agree with me. They sought to get over their initial grief so they could immerse themselves in the world and their "lives" —hoping to get back to a bit of what their lives were like before that terrible day.

Some had young children, and for them, devoting time to a group like ours quickly became something of a luxury. After all, children needed to be bathed, fed and driven to soccer and gymnastics. When there were children, there was often less time for reflection.

Still others left because they weren't ready to confront the horrible reality of how profoundly their lives had changed. Some simply were not in a good place emotionally. After all, we all brought to that day the whole of our personal histories. Some had experienced previous losses that made the current one more difficult to deal with.

And, as I mentioned, there were those who resented Mike simply because he had survived and their loved one did not. They revealed their feelings by showing disinterest in getting to know him. While the members of the group were warm to one another, some just ignored Mike or met his attempts at conversation curtly. Sometimes, there were whispered comments among the women when Mike shared his experiences.

But I saw that Mike walked through every day wrestling with the meaning of the many times he'd escaped death.

"I don't know why I'm here and others aren't," he said simply.

Mike wanted to try and find out. He tried hard through a variety of means to find meaning in his survival.

That determination made him and his wife, Amy, integral parts of our now-smaller group.

As the size of our group diminished, so did the frequency of our meetings. From once a week, to every two weeks, to once a month and then every two or three months. We seemed to sense when we needed to come together to discuss issues related to our lives and September 11th. In bumps and jerks, we were moving forward together and often found ourselves in similar emotional places at similar times.

For one meeting, I invited Harvey Kushner, the terrorism expert, to come and speak with us. In his remarks, he touched on a number of issues. Through him, we seemed to gain a sense of who these people were who had altered our lives so dramatically. He also helped us sort through whether we should sue the government, or whether we should apply for the September 11th Victim Compensation Fund. His experiences in dealing with families wrenched by major disaster helped each of us. His advice and his candor spoke to each of us in ways that we could not have imagined even a few short weeks earlier.

"There is no *right* choice," he made clear to us. There were only decisions, each with its own practical and emotional repercussions.

His manner and message put each of us in charge of our lives, and I appreciated that. I was ready to hear someone tell me that choosing option A would lead to certain consequences and that option B would lead to certain other consequences. Neither was right, neither was wrong. Each had upsides and each had downsides.

The choice was mine.

Some people felt powerless because of the choices. *What should I do?* they wondered. But I wanted the information and the power to choose. That was what I needed.

Harvey and I became good friends through the group. He arranged for me to speak on radio and television, sharing my story with others. In turn, I arranged for Harvey to speak at my synagogue about the threat of terrorism, which he is an expert at assessing. He was the chairperson of the Criminal Justice Department at C.W. Post College and a terrorist profiler for the United States government.

His talk was very well received at the synagogue, Jews being particularly sensitive to the threats that terrorism poses. Unfortunately, those of us who love Israel had seen how terrorists and their actions affected the lives and lifestyle of thousands of people—indeed, how the threat of terrorism could define a government's response to everyday events, just as the threat of terrorism had changed the way our U.S. government views the world today.

Through Harvey, I got to know Jami Gaudet, a radio talk-show host in Macon, Georgia. Imagine, me, a nice Jewish girl from Brooklyn, New York, getting to know and becoming friends with a talk-show personality from Macon, Georgia! Well, it happened. After a telephone interview, Jami invited me down to Georgia to speak live on her radio show—as well as at her synagogue on Rosh Hashanah.

One thing I learned from that experience was that people who suspected that the interest in what happened on September 11th diminished the further one traveled from New York or Washington were just plain wrong. They clung to such clichés as, "Out of sight, out of mind." If it doesn't happen to you, you forget about it after a while. But I found the opposite to be true.

I found that people all over the country were hungry to understand, to know, to vicariously experience what those of us closer to the attack had experienced. They felt the hurt, even if they didn't feel the noise of the explosion. Everywhere I traveled in Georgia, I found people who expressed their *personal* grief, anger and outrage about what had happened. Truly, what had happened that day happened to all Americans everywhere.

I was like a relic from the event. People wanted to see me. To touch me. To express their hurt to me and for me.

This was a powerful experience for me—this personal experience of bonding with Americans loving one another so directly and sensitively. It was plain that no one in this world had the right to take away another's right to stand upon this planet and live. No one should be able to determine how we live our lives.

I was so moved by all these experiences and these lessons that they became interwoven in the remarks I made on the first night of Rosh

Hashanah at Jami's synagogue. It was not until later that I began to realize that what I was really doing with my words was ringing in the Jewish New Year with a voice of hope.

Hope.

Where did I find hope? I don't know. To my mind, all I was doing was expressing my personal story of that terrible day. I shared with them my memories of my husband and the world that had disappeared for me that day.

I wanted those people to get to know Ira, because without knowing Ira, they could never get to know me.

"It was a terrible day, but I am here. My sons are here. And we are moving forward ... with our lives, with our love for one another and with our love for Ira."

The rabbi, in thanking me for my words, spoke of an ancient Jewish saying that "a man who brings children into the world is never dead."

How true those words were to me! Ira's voice, his words, his values, his joy remain alive in our sons. I can "hear" Ira when I hear them. I can "see" Ira when I see them.

I recognize the mannerisms that they have taken from him. The quick smiles. The passion for sports. The drive. The heart.

Bryan and Adam.

We are a different family without Ira, but the family Ira and I created continues on. It grows, and it grows stronger.

Like some of the others, my emotional needs, and emotional healing, meant that in some ways I was "outgrowing" the support group. Larry and Judy said that it was a positive sign, to be ready and able to move on. The WTC group had helped me deal with the shock of losing Ira, but it couldn't reach into my soul in the way I needed.

I needed support in mourning, so I sought a bereavement group—a group of people who understood the depth of the loss I was feeling. The members of the group were women who had also lost spouses at around my age and were willing to share experiences and help one another move forward.

There were times, in the darkest of the dark hours, that I was feeling so small and alone…and then a light would emerge. A flower would bloom. That was how I felt when I walked into the bereavement group. I had found a light, a place to flower and bloom.

Bereavement is a process that everyone who has lost someone goes through. Men and women. This particular bereavement group was composed only of women. The meetings began at the end of March—perfect timing for me. The days were starting to get longer. The weather was getting better. The roads were clearer—better for the forty-five minute drive to where the group met.

I walked in, tentative at first, and found a seat near Marge and Ilene. They had been to another bereavement group in the past and were hoping to have a better experience this time around. Others soon joined us. And then the social worker sat down. When I looked around the group, into the faces of the women gathered there, I was surprised.

What had I been expecting? A group made up of grandmothers? I don't know, but I do know I wasn't expecting to see a gathering of attractive, vibrant, intelligent women in their late forties and early fifties. As we went around the circle and introduced ourselves, it was clear to me that these women would find a way to go on to good, happy and productive lives. They had so much to offer.

It was at that moment I realized that I would go on to a good, happy and productive life, too. I was like these women. I was vibrant, intelligent, attractive.

I wasn't sure of the details as to *how* I was going to go about living a good and happy life. I just knew that I would. I would fill in the details as time went on. For the time being, I would have to make do with a little bit of *chutzpah*.

The social worker explained that we would work together to recognize our loss and work through our painful feelings and fears, coming to terms with our new lives as single women.

Single women. I could feel the cringe around the circle when she used that phrase. Not one of us had wanted to reach this point in our lives and find ourselves as "single women." Yet that was what we were.

"Bloom where you are planted," right?

We supported one another through our one-year anniversaries. Through birthdays. Through problems with children and other family members. We were there for one another during the unveilings and other difficult events. From out of that group, strong social bonds formed. We each knew that we'd always be able to count on one another.

We also knew that we would have to be strong and creative for one another. We had all had the assumptions we'd made about our lives change out from under us. So, we were there when Ilene's daughter, Rori, became a Bat Mitzvah. When, at the celebration, it was time to lift Ilene up in a chair, we sent the men away. Our group of women did it. We lifted each other up.

None of us is an island.

None of us can do it alone.

Our individual selves can only be found when we find ourselves with others.

CHAPTER TWENTY

Dating, Again?

Creating a new life is a lot like making soup from scratch. You put the ingredients together and season to taste.

This is how I went about creating myself as a single woman. I put the ingredients together and then seasoned to taste.

My basic ingredients were my family, my longtime friends, my job, my home. These were the familiar standbys. The soup stock, as it were. But the seasoning was going to have to be a lot spicier if I was going to be successful. In other words, I had to seek out new seasonings and new experiences to make my soup satisfying to the taste.

I was going to have to socialize more, get myself out of the house. But, in the past, socializing had always meant finding another couple to do something with—go out to eat, see a movie. Now, socializing meant something completely new. I was going to have to *date*!

Oy vey! I hadn't been out on a date since I was nineteen. Just the thought of going on a date was enough to give me a panic attack. And my kids were just *thrilled* to think of their mother traipsing out on dates.

Not that we had long conversations about it. Mom going out with other men is not much of a conversation starter with sons. But my sons were both adults, and they understood intellectually that my future meant meeting other people. They *wanted* that for me. At least they did intellectually. They didn't want me to be alone, and they certainly didn't want me to be unhappy.

But dealing with the reality of your mother going out on dates was another thing entirely. Imagine bumping into them when I was at a movie. How awkward would that be?

Of course, the likelihood of that happening was slim. Bryan didn't live nearby, and Adam was getting ready to move out of the house. Still, the mental image was enough to give them—and me—pause.

What they actually said was, "Do what you want. I don't want to know about it."

Part of me had to chuckle. Talk about role reversal! How many nights had I prayed to God that they were behaving well and that they came home safe and sound? Being a parent is a great deal of "don't ask, don't tell." But now, it turned out that being a child was going to be a lot of that, too.

Well, so be it.

During this period of time, when I was seriously contemplating dating but hadn't quite gotten to the actual dating, I often had imaginary conversations in which I pictured what I would suggest to Ira if he were in my position. How would I tell him to get on with his life?

Knowing Ira, he would probably play paddleball and eat pizza on weekends, with friends encouraging him to get out there and go out and have a good time. His friends at work would go out with him, because he spent so much time there. People would start introducing him to women, telling him that it "was time."

Once out there, he would discover that, hey, this isn't so bad. In my imagination, the supply of women would be never-ending. Young women. Older women. Casserole bearers. Dinner inviters.

Thinking about it never failed to make me smile, picturing Ira with that long line of women.

However, I would soon come out of my reverie and remember that it was *me* who was alive. I was the one who had to face the reality of moving on.

I guess a good portion of my hesitance was that I was so lucky with Ira. He was a romantic who was very devoted to me. He loved birds and always reminded me that eagles mated for life. When a cardinal appeared outside our window, darting from branch to branch, he would shout excitedly for me to come to the window.

"Look, look at that!

It was beautiful. So was his excitement and enthusiasm.

He was a big reason I would be able to move on—and a huge reason that I would never be able to settle for a sparrow. How could I ever settle for a mere flitting bird when I had soared with an eagle?

CHAPTER TWENTY-ONE

Teachers Around Me

On one hand, what was the big deal about dating? You meet someone. Have dinner. Go to a movie. No big deal. Right? Just the thought of it filled me with chills. No doubt about it, dating appeared to be tough. How could it not be? If I was being honest, it wasn't all that easy when I was nineteen. It sure wasn't going to be easier now.

In this, as in all other things, I realized that I was just going to have to reorganize my life and my way of thinking. I was used to loving one man my entire life. Dating was superficial compared to what I'd shared with Ira.

It was definitely going to take some getting used to.

I had spent so many special days with Ira, more than I could count. And now, every day, a specific day or special moment would pop into my thoughts. How could dinner and a movie stand up to those things?

One special day we'd enjoyed together was when we went to the New York Botanical Gardens and saw a special panel discussion of *The Lion King* by its writers and producers. I found the entire discussion fascinating, learning how a tremendous production was put on, from start to finish.

One of the writers said something that day that has always stuck with me. He said that creating a show was like "making soup." After the audience finished chuckling at the comment, he went on, "I'm serious. Just like soup. You put it together and adjust the ingredients."

For a play, that meant the book, the actors, the music, the choreographers, the money people, the stage, etc. For a life … well, it meant a good deal more than that. But putting together a life was a daunting task.

Thinking of a life as making soup helped. Putting together soup? Well, that was something I could handle.

In my mind's eye, I could see my mother and her mother standing in their kitchens making soup, and the image comforted me. I would smile as I pictured them adding a pinch of this and a dash of that.

They were strong women, competent women, and had passed their strengths along to me. In fact, from the day my mother went back to work when I was fourteen, I realized I had been "making soup." I loved feeling independent without my mother looking over my shoulder. Knowing that I could create my own schedule, as long as I fulfilled my responsibilities at home, felt good.

I shared my mother's love of cooking and got dinner into the oven every day. It was fun for me to "take over" at home until my mother returned from work. I enjoyed creating my own schedule for studying and socializing. Having a working mother fostered my independence in my adolescence.

I was just going to have to assert those strengths once again.

My family obligations are now more emotional than physical. No more shopping, cooking, carpooling and overseeing homework. My sons are grown men who need occasional emotional support. I am independent and ready to face the future. My life soup has new ingredients, some of which are new to me—and a bit frightening—while others are as familiar as my mother's kitchen.

Making life soup brings me back to Deepak Chopra. I often think of that meditation he'd shared with me over the radio that long-ago morning. "Who am I? What do I want?"

Whoever would have thought that Deepak was talking about soup!?

Who *am* I? What *do* I want?

I want to speak out. I want to share. I want to inspire. I want to touch lives.

Throughout my life, I have always operated "behind the scenes." I have been a wife. A mother. A teacher. Helping others move closer to their dreams. And, if September 11th had never happened, if Ira was alive today and by my side, I would be more than content to have continued on that path. Nothing would have made me happier than being able to remain with him, loving him, retiring with him.

I would have pursued the things I enjoyed, like writing, but without the deep pain of losing Ira. Why? Because nothing dramatic enough had occurred in my life to inspire this deep passion.

September 11th changed that.

Now I want … no, now I *need* to speak out. Now I need to encourage people to respect one another. I need to help people see that life *can* be win-win and not "I can only win if you lose."

I want the passion to continue Ira's love in the world. As difficult as this path has been, I believe that I am on it for a reason. Wasn't it Martin Luther King, Jr., who said, "It's not the outrageousness of the small minority but the apathy of the majority," that should occupy our concerns?

I want to grab that majority by its shirt collar and shake it into action.

John Lennon captured my feeling in his beautiful song "Imagine."

You may say I'm a dreamer
But I'm not the only one.
I hope someday you'll join us
And the world will live as one.

Music has had such a profound impact on my life. On all of our lives. So many of our songwriters and singers have communicated such powerful truths to us. Marvin Gaye was another, in his song "Mercy Mercy Me."

Whoa, ah, mercy, mercy me

Ah, things ain't what they used to be
Where did all the blue skies go?
Poison is the wind that blows
From the north and south and east

There are teachers all around us. We need to open our ears to their lessons.

I want to be one of those kinds of teachers.

CHAPTER TWENTY-TWO

Alone

A friend of mine, another teacher, always used to marvel when she would see her students five, seven, even ten years after they'd been in her classroom. "They don't really change," she said. "Not really."

Another friend of mine, a nursery school director, made a similar observation. "You can see a child's nature very early, and for the most part, that nature doesn't change much. Oh, the shy one might overcome the shyness enough to speak in public, or to play music. But for the most part, that is just maximizing other strengths. Basic natures don't change much."

I think a more insightful observation was made by another colleague who noted that the adage, "The apple doesn't fall far from the tree," was generally a sound rule. "Except," he noted, "in the event of a dramatic life change. Or," he added somewhat sadly, "if the child begins to drink or abuse drugs."

When I pursued his thinking about what "changes" a person, he said that he had seen young people changed by the early death of a loved one, or a dramatic shift in the financial situation of the family.

"Unfortunately, most of the time these abrupt changes are caused by tragic events. I would guess that winning the lottery could have the same effect."

Or, I thought to myself, *finding love or gaining a spiritual insight.*

I believe that people can and do change. But I also recognize that we confront life with some basic strengths and weaknesses that are with us pretty much from our early childhoods. Put another way, our personal "cupboards" can have slightly different ingredients for our lives' soup.

Someone who is a pessimist would have a harder time when confronted with a tragedy than someone who is an optimist. Generally speaking. For an optimist, a tragedy could alter his or her basic worldview.

There are a great many variables. But we must remember that we, as people, as human beings, bring a great many strengths to the table. Each of us and all of us. We have the potential for creativity, for intelligence, for love.

Dealing with a tragedy is never a simple, straightforward process. It is a wild roller coaster of emotions, of demands, of fears and hopes.

I have been fortunate to have a very optimistic nature. I have always seen the glass as being "half full." Whenever Ira would worry about things at work or at home, I was the one who helped him see the bright side. I was the one always looking for silver linings, the one to counsel perspective. "A career is only a career. We have a life and a family…"

I could almost hear my mother and my grandmother saying, "As long as you have your health…" I understand now that they meant health as the starting point, that with health you have possibilities—opportunities to achieve goals with an unencumbered self.

But I would be less than truthful if I made it sound like I was always looking for the silver linings after September 11th. Anyone who suggests that any of us—the ones who suffered the loss of loved ones—has managed well would not be telling the truth.

Even now, after that horrible morning, I know the feeling of waking up and feeling I am in the bottom of a very black hole. Life can be very tough. Because the loss of my husband is a constant reality. Every day brings its own challenges and changes that are added on top of that reality.

You see, the world does not stop turning. People have to begin to deal with their lives and issues. Even my sons, who shared with me a terrible loss, have to move on.

They lost their father.

They were not widowed.

Bryan had to turn his attention to his family and building his career. Adam had to begin his life even as I had to begin my life anew. As a recent college graduate, he was tasked with finding the "right job." I know how much my sons care about me, but they have to concern themselves with their lives first and foremost. That is what I want for them.

But that doesn't mean it's not hard.

I was fortunate that Adam still lived at home when the terrorists struck. Having him there day after day was a comfort beyond anything I can describe. Not only was he there for me, but because he was there, I knew that I had to concern myself with his feelings. I could more easily be outward thinking. But now, Adam has moved out to forge his independent life, finding an apartment and a room-mate. And although that was "supposed to happen," it meant another change for me, an empty house. And once more, the magnitude of my loss was inescapable.

Memories are my constant companion and, while often comforting, they also are constant reminders of what was and what can no longer be. And what will never be again.

Before September 11th, I would look at old photographs, and I would "miss" Adam and Bryan as small boys. But that was mostly nostalgia. I could miss my young children but appreciate the young men they had become and how much I enjoyed their place in my life. Now, I struggle with something more than nostalgia. This feeling, this loss, a wrenching in the center of my being. I can feel it like a tight knot in my stomach and a gripping in my throat.

How I miss those winter weekends when Ira and I would wander out during the day and then spend a cozy evening at home! It is painful to know that those winters are gone. My solace, and it is a great one, is that now I can do whatever I want. I am also fortunate to be young enough to enjoy that vast new freedom.

But it is tough. One day, I was married. The next, I was a widow. Just like that. Every aspect of my life has taken on a new dimension and meaning. There is nothing that has not changed, from the trivial to the significant, from the arrangement of my clothes in the closet and the drawers that are now available to me, to how I occupy my bed.

I find that I am also a good deal more sensitive in ways that I never was before. If I had an informal arrangement to meet with a close colleague for "a bite" or at a clothing store or for a few minutes, and they became distracted or forgot or their life intruded, I would feel a little hurt and neglected. Dates and phone calls with close friends meant more to me than before. Friends were now my closest connections and my comfort.

In the past, I would have shrugged off those kinds of disappointments easily. After all, Ira was always at home waiting for me. I had that secure relationship there waiting for me. I had a home base.

No more.

There is an irony about this realization that I recognize. Growing up when I did, I read Camus. I read Sartre. It was easy then to say, "We are all alone. Man lives his life alone and dies alone." But that was an intellectual acknowledgment. It wasn't a fundamental awareness of the real thing.

I was raised during a time when I was given the language to describe being alone but never before had I experienced the depth of that aloneness. I had never known the texture of it, the quality of it, the dangers of it or the pain of it.

Now, I saw myself moving through my life as a solitary player. I came home from work. I walked my dog. I ate a little dinner. I did a few things around the house. I went to sleep.

All alone.

Oh, I knew that I was surrounded by friends and family who cared about me deeply. But they did not live with me.

I was alone.

But in that aloneness, I could already feel the first stirrings of growth. Like the first green shoots to appear on the slopes of Mount St. Helens after the violent eruption, there was life under the layer of gray and ash. There was a seedling ready to flourish and a flower preparing to bloom.

I could already feel myself nurturing that green shoot growing in my soul. I knew that I must work through this time in order to free myself from the feelings that held me back. I believed that I would. I knew that I would.

There were many ironies in my circumstances. Having been an avid and relatively intelligent reader with a desire to write creatively, I always believed that the best work, the work of the soul, was produced by people who were able to be alone with themselves.

Well, now, eighteen months after 9/11, I was alone. Could I produce?

I now had uninterrupted time at my beck and call. There was no one making demands of me or my time. Could I turn my attention to the passions in my soul? Could I nurture the flower that will blossom where it is planted?

These were daunting questions. Scary ones. Good ones. Very good ones. I always told my students that there were no "stupid" questions, only good ones. Well, these were very good ones.

I had begun to think of this process, of coming to terms with my aloneness and individuality, as part of the healing process that I must go through—indeed, that everyone who suffered a loss on that morning must go through. What our nation must go through.

On one level, I have been given a great gift. I have been given the opportunity—okay, this opportunity has been unwelcome and thrust upon me, but it is an opportunity nonetheless—to rediscover me.

I am involved in a great expedition. A grand excavation. I am like an archaeologist at a site that has the promise of revealing the secrets and the mysteries of the ancient world. I look at myself in the mirror and I am like that archaeologist gazing upon a meadow. What is there looks familiar and uncompelling, but underneath there is a treasure trove that far exceeds the tomb of King Tut!

My task is to muster the courage to begin to dig. To take my metaphorical shovel and trowel, and burrow beneath the familiar surface to the secrets below.

Yes, this is an opportunity and a gift. (I guess I *do* still look for silver linings!) My sons are functioning on their own. I am no longer a "wife." I am just me. Felice.

It's time for Felice to emerge unencumbered by other life roles, no longer defined by other people's needs and expectations. It's time for Felice to do something wonderful with her life to help herself and to inspire others.

Marianne Williamson, in her book *A Return to Love*, wrote the following:

Our deepest fear is not that we are inadequate. Our deepest fear is that we are powerful beyond measure. It is our light, not our darkness, that most frightens us. We ask ourselves, "Who am I to be brilliant, gorgeous, talented, fabulous?" Actually, who are you not to be? You are a child of God. Your playing small does not serve the world. There is nothing enlightened about shrinking so that other people won't feel insecure around you. We were born to make manifest the glory of God that is within us. It is not just in some of us; it is in everyone. And as we let our own light shine, we unconsciously give permission to other people to do the same. As we are liberated from our own fear, our presence automatically liberates others.

That is the green shoot that I saw emerging from this terrible event. That is how I could give meaning to my loss.

Which is the only way any of us can find silver linings in the clouds of our lives—by finding meaning in the clouds themselves.

CHAPTER TWENTY-THREE

The Me Project

One day in the winter of 2003, I was feeling down and lonely. After allowing myself a few minutes of sadness, I "took hold" of myself and tried to think of things I could do to lift myself out of the blue emotions I was feeling. It wasn't easy. I just felt as though September 11th had just happened, and I couldn't see a way to move forward.

"You're not the same person you were then," I told myself.

But I didn't seem to be buying my determined argument. So, I decided to "convince" myself of all the progress I'd made since that horrible day. I created a timeline of my accomplishments over the course of the preceding year or so. By the time I was finished, not only was I feeling a bit more in control of my feelings, but I was also very impressed with myself.

Not only had I taken care of all the financial loose ends related to Ira's tragic death, but I had made many new friends, had traveled to many places and begun to immerse myself in new activities. And, I had dated four men.

Four men!

Looking over the short list of names, it looked anything but short to me. I found it amazing that I had somehow gotten myself "out there" again. If someone had said to me before September 11th that I would be dating again soon, I would have said they were crazy. And if someone had said to me during the first few months after September 11th that I'd be dating again, I'd have said they were crazy.

And if they had said that I'd have dated *four* men by this point, I'd have said they were crazy times four. But there it was, in black and white on the paper I was writing on. Four men. Each with a name, a personality and shtick.

I couldn't help but smile to myself. Dating was concrete evidence that I had committed to establishing a new life for myself, that I was firmly rooted in the present and the future and not lost in the past.

Each of the men I had gone out with had been exceptionally nice people, but there was only one with whom I felt any kind of "chemistry." However, having been an English major in college, I knew that there was more to life than chemistry. This man had other issues that made any real relationship improbable, despite the chemistry.

"So, do you like dating?" one of my friends asked me.

Do I like dating? Hmm, that's not an easy question to answer. I wish I didn't have to be dating, that's for sure. But I do like that panicky, nervous anticipation that comes before a date—at fifty-three years old, just like it did at nineteen!

In some ways, dating is no different for me now than it was then. You meet someone you find interesting. You go out. You like him, or you're disappointed and you laugh about the whole insanity of it with your friends. (Did I really write that? How old am I anyway?)

The issue of sexuality is different now. The world is different. And I am different. But dating... well, that's very much the same. And I like that I feel comfortable enough with myself as a person to get myself out there and enjoy (or try to enjoy) whatever experiences I can. And the process, dating, has given me real hope that I will find an appropriate, compatible partner again one day.

Dating has raised some other interesting issues. Meeting new men, and viewing them as potential partners rather than acquaintances or friends, has given me a fresh perspective on my relationship with Ira. Thinking back, I'm wondering if Ira and I were so compatible during those early years.

Remember that wonderful song "Do You Love Me?" from *Fiddler on the Roof*? I love that song and that scene, because in many ways it expresses a reality that every married couple experiences. Although our marriage had not been arranged, Ira and I approached it like every other couple—virtual strangers to one another.

How could any two people, two individuals, hope to make a life together in such an intimate way as marriage calls for? What Ira and I learned was that we *wanted* to be together, even when we were a bit confused as to how to make that work. So, what did we do? We concentrated on finding a way. We worked on our relationship. And we built a life in which we had wonderful things in common.

My relationship with Ira was built upon raising a family together. There were, of course, a great many other things. But that was our bedrock. Our foundation.

Well, not being nineteen anymore and not wishing to revisit my childbearing years again, I did not anticipate any new relationship to be built upon the same foundation. It would have to be built upon something else.

But what? What exactly might that "something else" be? Certainly I want my next partner to "have it together," but what will that mean?

That he is comfortable with himself? That he is settled? That his children are grown? What if he's divorced? Will that "baggage" be different than if he's widowed?

I certainly want to find someone I find attractive. A person I can communicate with on all levels and someone who has had or who can understand a real "family experience." But all that is not enough. I want someone who is greater than the sum of all the parts.

Perhaps I need to find someone with whom I share common goals. Or maybe I will need to find someone who can relate to my experience in losing Ira, someone who has suffered through adversity and has learned how to rebuild a life after his dreams had been shattered.

And maybe these ruminations are just a reaction to this particular point in my recovery from September 11th, and in another six months they will seem childish. I can't say. All I can do is be glad that I have not gotten too involved in a relationship yet. I know I am still evolving. My thinking is changing so rapidly when it comes to this and so many other things!

When I look for "signposts" along this particular path in life, I seek out people who have gone through experiences such as mine. For instance, I admire Katie Couric a great deal. Having lost her husband at a young age to colon cancer, she was left a widow with two young girls to raise.

What did she do? Well, one thing she did was to take her tragedy and face it head on so others would benefit. She dedicated herself to work that would benefit cancer research. She has also had a televised colonoscopy to encourage everyone to understand the disease that killed her husband and some of the steps that make it eminently preventable.

Added to this loss, she lost her sister as well in 2001—yet she continued to be successful at NBC. I cheered when I read that she had a new boyfriend.

I still cheer for her. I hope she continues to face the future successfully. Because I know in my heart that if she can, and if others like her can, then I can, too. And if I can, then you can, too.

So, now I am confronted with what it means, really, to be fulfilled. "Fulfilled." Like so many other ideas, it turns out I had placed a great deal of credence in what had essentially been just a word to me. An idea. But now, to be fulfilled is a real, day-to-day, concrete goal. It is not a pie-in-the-sky idea. It is necessary. It is practical.

It is real.

So, what does it mean to me to be fulfilled?

In the past, I could have answered that question easily. Having a family and a career. If those two things were in place, then I was satisfied. But now, with my husband gone and my sons grown and my career beyond question, it is not so easy to answer the question about fulfillment.

Now, the answer is all tied up in "self-actualization." In other words, the answer is not about something outside of me, it is about me and everything within me.

I am the project that I need to be working on right now. And yet, I do want another loving man in my life. But now, a loving man, a partner, will have to be a full partner. Someone I can work with to do good in this world.

I want my next partner to have many goals in common with me. I want him to help me find what makes me happy.

CHAPTER TWENTY-FOUR

Recalibrating

It is easy to look back and see the past as having been perfect. Seen through the lens of the tragedy of September 11th, it is hard to see Ira as anything but a perfect husband and father. It is hard to think that there was anything less than perfect about our relationship.

Of course, it is ridiculous to think that things were "perfect" in the past. No one's life is ever perfect. And I would be less than honest if I didn't admit to having regrets even as far back as when I first married Ira.

You see, I had never lived on my own as a single, independent woman. I went directly from my parents' house to living with Ira. I missed out completely on that period of self-discovery and adventure that many young women enjoy during their early twenties.

Well, guess what? I might have "missed the boat" during my early twenties, but the boat found me during my early fifties. Not knowing what the future will bring is a bit scary, but also exciting.

Not that it is easy to get used to relying on yourself. When you're used to having at least one person shouldering more than half of your life for thirty years, it's hard to simply reverse course and take over by yourself. Of course, the deal is, there is no choice. You do what you have to do.

Easier said than done, naturally. During the long, cold winter days following September 11th, I would often remain indoors. Nesting? Perhaps. But for a woman who had been a social creature her entire life, I missed the sound of another's voice. I missed the closeness of having other people around. I felt the solitude profoundly.

I knew that I had to restructure my time if I was going to make it through those long days. After all, Ira and I, like any other couple, had a rhythm to our lives, routines that we followed as a couple. Without those routines, I felt like I had lost my rhythm. Especially on the weekends, when there seemed to be nothing but time spread out before me. I used to look forward to long weekends, when Ira and I could spend time together. Now, I had to work to make sure the time was filled with other activities, with other family members and with friends.

I also had to take on responsibilities that had always been Ira's. The financial matters. Simple household chores, like changing the outside light bulbs. If a repair was required, I either had to figure out a way to do it or arrange for a repair person to come in to take care of it.

And, in addition to the practical matters, there were emotional peaks and valleys to contend with. All part of the grieving process, but no less difficult because of it.

I have had people tell me that a year is long enough to grieve. As though there is an appropriate time limit on grief. That is absolutely false. The notion of the "year" seems to come from the Jewish tradition of setting the tombstone in place after a year; but this is to commemorate the end of public grief, it in no way suggests that private grief ends. Not only is a single year not nearly enough time, but the suggestion that such an emotional struggle has to fit a time frame is insulting at best.

Many professionals point out that it takes two to three years to grieve successfully for a spouse or parent, two to three years before one can reorganize their life and restructure their world.

Certainly that has been my situation. It wasn't even until the second year that I really experienced the true aloneness of my situation. And the permanency of Ira's loss. There were times when it was frightening. Yet I coped. I made it my business to make firm plans to fill in the time on weekends.

Soon, I began to enjoy my time alone. And I discovered a remarkable reality. I *liked* myself. Really and truly.

I was discovering genuine perspective, on myself, on my life, on my relationship with Ira, on my hopes for the future. In short, I was discovering *me*. And I was enjoying the process. I was in no hurry to muck it up by making "me" a "we" by entering into a relationship that I wasn't ready for. I knew better than to rush into anything.

After all, what I want in a partner is evolving all the time. If I had entered into a relationship too soon, I would likely have found someone as much like Ira as possible. And while that might have been comforting in the short term, what I want in the long term is something a bit different. Yes, I want someone who will care for me as much as Ira did, but my next partner and I will have a relationship built upon a different foundation and with different goals.

And the last thing I need in a relationship is for it to be built on a foundation of fear of being alone, or some other deep negativity.

And, I continue to have a relationship with Ira. I do believe in an afterlife. I believe the soul ascends to other levels after the body dies. I also think that if we grieve too long and too hard, the soul of the deceased is weighted down. When grief is successful and genuine, the soul is freed to move on.

So how I behave and how I find self-realization has a great deal to do with Ira and for Ira. In a deep way, we are still in this together. It's just that now I am the one who must make all the decisions and choices.

CHAPTER TWENTY-FIVE

A New Path

So, where to from here? This part of my journey began on September 11, 2001, but it has now gone on and on, in a positive direction.

There are people who ask me, "Aren't you angry?" or "How can you deal with your terrible loss?"

People want to know if I am happy about our current war on terrorism.

Some days, I do cheer our resolve to root out terror and save others from the horror I have experienced. By the same token, I am not blind to the suffering that our fighting brings to the lives of innocent people in many countries. Not to mention the danger the fighting poses to the young men and women who proudly wear the uniform of the United States of America.

Remember, as a teacher in a diverse community, I have had Muslim children in my classroom before and after September 11th. One day, a day when I was feeling particularly sad, I happened to have a discussion with one of these students. He explained to me the meaning of *hajj,* of pilgrimage to Mecca. As he spoke, I could see a light in his eyes, a wonderful, positive light that spoke of all things good about faith and none of the bad and painful.

My student is living proof that goodness is everywhere, just as evil can be.

So, am I angry? No. I cannot hold on to anger. That is too negative and damaging to me and solves nothing of the wrongs that caused

September 11th. And it would not honor Ira's memory. He would never be like that.

There are days when it seems that he is still everywhere. Days when I "see" him as I watch couples go into the supermarket together. I can see him in the driver's seat of the car. I can hear his laugh. I feel as if I could reach out and actually touch him.

But, of course, I can't. Ira is everywhere with me and nowhere. On days when I really feel his presence, I doubt that I could ever love another person the way that I loved him. But then I think that I could love another man, but differently. That's all. Differently. No future relationship could take away from what I had with Ira.

I have lost the love of my youth, the love I grew up with. I have lost the love I invested my heart and my life in, thinking that we would have... if not forever, then certainly many, many more happy years together. I pictured us being one of those couples who celebrated a fiftieth wedding anniversary surrounded by children, grandchildren and friends.

But that was not the way God planned it. Now I am left to carry on alone. I have a new path now and I, rather than we, am the anchor for my family.

In February of 2003, I wrote Ira a letter about a very special man that I'd met.

Dear Ira,

I have met a very interesting man. This guy is different from the others. He is brilliant and compassionate. Having experienced personal tragedy himself, he understands where I am coming from and believes, like I do, that the way to reconcile his loss is through love and forgiveness. This man is a person of action and is working to bring more light into the world by helping those in need to overcome their circumstances and succeed in life. He has a deep respect for human life.

This man learned all about our family before we met in person and impressed me with his insights and the fact that he cared enough to develop insights. Ira, he and I are planning to work together based on our common ideology. I am sure that through this work, we will continue your love in the world. In the face of anger, hatred and destruction, your love will continue to grow on this earth.

I love you forever.

In my mind, I asked Ira what he thought about this new relationship. I saw him holding his hands up in a enthusiastic cheer. That told me that I was heading in the right direction. Actually, I already knew that, but it's nice to know he approves.

I know the "right" guy will understand that I will always love Ira very much. He will not be threatened by that. The man I referred to in the letter understood. I think he even appreciated me more because he knew how deeply I can love.

I hope he is right.

There is doubt. Of course, there is doubt. But I am moving forward. As Ralph Waldo Emerson said, "Do not go where the path may lead, go instead where there is no path and leave a trail."

I can feel all my nerve endings being alive with electricity. I am alive. I am alone, but I am alive. I am filled with experience and potential. The world is there, waiting for me.

A month after I wrote that letter, I had a recurrence of the dream that I believe reveals the deep excitement I feel for the future and my new life, despite the moments of fear and sadness. In my dream, I was on my way to my teaching job, but I was running late so I turned down a new street. I looked around and found I liked this street very much. There were people on the sidewalk that I wanted to talk to. There were stores and new places, interesting places, that captured my attention.

But I knew I had to get to work, so I stopped to ask directions. I was given directions, but it was clear that I had gone a long way from my destination and that it would take me a long while to get to school. So I called the school on my phone.

The secretary answered and, after listening to my explanation, said simply, "You can't continue to be late every day, dear."

I felt guilty for being late, yet I was fascinated by this new place that seemed to have been hidden from me my entire life.

Yes, I think this dream is very telling. I'm ready to explore. To branch out. To experience the world in all its beauty and variation.

I am a woman in transition.

I am on my way.

Not long ago, I was listening to the radio when the personality began talking about a poet. The poet's wife had died, and after her death all of his poetry was about how much he missed her and what her death meant to him. But then, after a few years, he began to write poetry about other things, things he'd always written about. He discovered love again. He had stopped mourning.

He was a poet transformed, just as I am a woman in the process of transformation. That is the lesson I have learned from September 11th. It was not an easy or welcome lesson, but it is an important one. We are all in the process of transformation.

And that is how we go "from here." For we are all always in the process of going forward. None of us has reached the end of our path.

Each of us as individuals, and all of us together, are walking along paths of transformation and transition.

Recognizing that is the first step.

Acknowledgments

Thank you to the Temple Hillel community of North Woodmere, to the Lawrence Public Schools community, to my friends and neighbors of the Five Towns, Long Island, New York, and to Ira's colleagues and friends at Lehman Brothers for their support of my family and me.

Thank you to Harvey Kushner for his wise counsel on managing the aftermath of 9/11, and to Jami Gaudet for conducting my first on-air interview and inviting me to share my story with her community in Macon, Georgia.

Thank you to David Woolfe who helped me create my original manuscript in 2002–2003. To my daughter-in-law, Natalie, for connecting me to Professor Elie Wiesel, who encouraged me to "circulate" my book around. Gratitude to Anthony Lerro, my first reader and fellow adventurer, and to Christine Reilly Cecot for her helpful edits and encouragement.

Appreciation to my many teachers and colleagues in the Certificate in Positive Psychology and Happiness Studies Academy programs, and the Let Your Yoga Dance community, for their spiritual and scientific teachings. I've learned so much from you. Thank you to Pedro Pacheco, my painting teacher, for encouraging me to express who I am in my artwork.

To Rabbi Harold Kushner for his wise life advice and his encouragement to get my book published my way.

To Sharon Epstein for generously sharing her writing/publishing journey. To my wonderful editor/book designer, Erica Schultz

Yakovetz, for her patience, creative design, and skillful editing, and to Sheri ArbitalJacoby for her careful final proofreading.

Most recently, I thank the print department at Staples in Valley Stream, New York, for their patience and technological support.

To my parents, I thank you for loving me unconditionally. I hope I've made you proud. And Grandma Dora for her validating winks.

To Mr. Yuni, my fifth-grade teacher who brought out his students' unique talents. I will always remember your encouragement of my writing.

And finally, to my family, I thank you for filling my heart with love and joy.